RAILWAY MODELLING

An Introduction by
W A Corkill

Illustrated with line drawings by the author
and with photographs by J. C. Coles ARPS unless
otherwise credited

David & Charles
Newton Abbot London   North Pomfret (Vt)

British Library Cataloguing in Publication Data
Corkill, W A
Railway Modelling
1. Railroads-Models
I. Title
625.19   TF197
ISBN 0-7153-7571-7

Library of Congress Catalog Card Number 78–52176

First published 1979
Second impression 1979

©W. A. Corkill 1979

Set by Quad Typesetters Limited
and printed in Great Britain
by Biddles Limited of Guildford
for David & Charles (Publishers) Limited
Brunel House Newton Abbot Devon

Published in the United States of America
by David & Charles Inc
North Pomfret Vermont 05053 USA

CONTENTS

Introduction   4

1   Policies and plans   5

2   Specifications   12

3   At the drawing board   19

4   Foundations   28

5   Trackwork and power supply   35

6   Civil Engineering   46

7   Scenery   57

8   Real Estate   61

9   Signals and automatic controls   68

10   Locomotives and rolling stock   77

11   Finishing touches   83

12   Operation and maintenance   86

Appendix 1: Graphical methods for scaling   88

Appendix 2: Electrical supplies and controls   90

Bibliography   94

Abbreviations   95

Index   96

A gauge O scale model of GWR 4-6-0 No 2912 *Saint Ambrose*, constructed at a Rugby training school. *J. Brown*

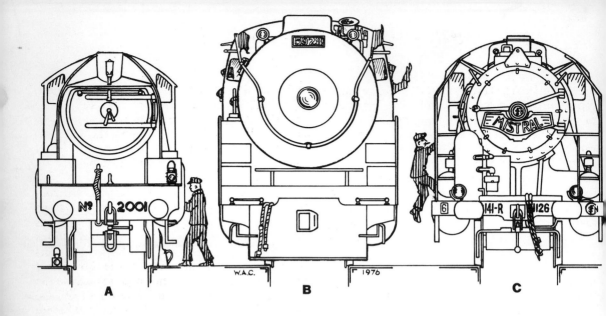

A   B   C

INTRODUCTION

Many boys of my generation had an ambition to become engine-drivers when they grew up, but most of them compromised and gave expression to this aim by operating gauge O Hornby tin-plate train sets. They then transferred their affections to fast cars, girl friends and other ruinously expensive hobbies while I stuck to railway modelling and found it to be a source of ever-increasing interest.

I think it all started with an appointment at the dentist's in 1935; or shortly afterwards when I was compensated with a visit to King's Cross station. The new streamlined Silver Jubilee train was there, and so was Gresley's apple-green masterpiece No 2001 *Cock O' The North*, designed on his return from trials of enormous Canadian Pacific locomotives in the Rockies. The driver invited me to occupy his cab seat, an honour which I readily accepted in a delightful atmosphere of smoke, steam, and hot oil vapour.

Some of the experience picked up in travels around Britain and abroad, and in my earlier attempts at modelling 'something different', were described in magazine articles in 1961–4 and modellers still occasionally write about them, asking for further information. They will, I am sure, find something of interest in this book,

whether they intend to follow British practice (as most of them will), Continental or North American, historical, modern or freelance, in large or small scales and gauges, with or without extensive scenery, signals and controls.

I have endeavoured to survey the whole hobby in just sufficient depth to enable the beginner to appreciate the great variety of available opportunities and the experienced modeller to consider new techniques or fields perhaps hitherto unexplored.

To all who have assisted in the preparation of this book, especially Dr P. Moore of the Southern Railways Group, who cast his eagle eye over the manuscript and offered many helpful suggestions, I gratefully acknowledge my indebtedness; as for those who have had the patience to read this far, I sincerely hope you will travel further with me into the fascinating world of railway modelling.

All aboard; Join the train, please!; *Bitte einsteigen; En voiture, s'il vous plaît; Attention au depart!*

And may your short circuits and your derailments be few and far between!

W. A. Corkill

CHAPTER ONE

POLICIES AND PLANS

Since World War II railway modelling has developed into such a popular hobby that the choice of commercially available equipment is almost bewildering. Most good model shops stock wide ranges of British, North American and Continental European type models in almost every scale and gauge. There are trends towards greater interest in modelling foreign as well as home railways and a more rapid spread of new ideas and techniques.

In the early days of model railways the popular scales and gauges were large enough to favour live steam locomotives running on garden tracks, or around spacious attics. Clockwork and electric motors presented less fire risk and required less maintenance, so they were progressively developed until the hobby split into model engineering for live steam devotees and the larger gauges, and railway modelling for followers of the smaller scales in which live steam was inappropriate. As smaller electric motors became commercially practicable, the range of scales

Fig 1 *(Opposite):* Three powerful locomotives drawn to the same scale (as described in Chapter Two); **A**, LNER P2 2-8-2 No 2001 *Cock O' The North.* **B**, CPR T-1-b Selkirk 2-10-4. **C**, *SNCF* 141 R 2-8-2.

Fig 2 A good start can be made with inexpensive plastic-bodied models like this GWR 4-2-2. Magnetised driving wheels give it improved adhesion on plated steel rails.

and gauges increased until the one time smallest, gauge O, was joined by smaller ones still in OO and HO in the years between the wars, OOO, N and TT, and finally Z during the last two decades. The commercial development of N gauge, particularly, has been most marked in recent years.

This volume is devoted to electrically-driven trains in all scales and gauges from gauge 1 down to Z, and to the layouts on which they run. It is divided into chapters dealing with definitions and techniques of easily distinguishable aspects of modelling, but reference is made throughout the text to layouts or scenes which illustrate the relevant principles in widely differing situations. These, which readers may care to glance at before getting down to technical particulars, range from simple groupings of inexpensive and easily obtainable models, figures 7, 9, 50 and 91, to more elaborate and advanced examples against which they may measure their ambitions and skills throughout their modelling careers. Features which give each of them an individual character will be described, but the fundamental principles are universal and international. References to scale and gauge should be read in conjunction with Chapter Two where newcomers to model railways will find the various sizes and terminology explained.

Fig 3 LMS 7P 4-6-2 No 6256 *Sir William A. Stanier, FRS* by the sheds on Mr J. Brown's gauge O layout, for which he made the baseboards, the track and the buildings.
J. Brown

Fig 4 Complicated kit-built trackwork (as described in Chapter Five) at Mr Brown's Bridgewater station.

Fig 5 Ex-GCR Director class 4-4-0 No 5434 *The Earl of Kerry* on a Sheffield train at Bridgewater.
J. Brown

Manchester Bridgewater (4) is an example of modelling by Mr J. Brown of the Gauge O Guild. Designed for eventual transfer to a garden layout, the baseboards, track and controls are robust but portable – in the wider sense of the word. It contains much interesting trackwork with stud-contact type current collection (133) and forms an excellent background for attractive pre-nationalisation locomotives and rolling stock. The location is an imaginary one but the policy is to use only equipment that *could* have worked into the station over the LMS lines from Stockport and Crewe or the LNER from Guide Bridge and Sheffield.

East Croydon is a real place on the main London-Brighton line of the Southern Region. The station was built by the LBSCR, which became part of the SR in 1923, and Peter Moore, who built this fine model, visited it often in his youth to take photographs and draw plans. Many of his records date from the 1930s, and those who know their Southern Railway will find evidence to suggest that his excellent layout represents the period of 1938–42. Styles of

painting and lettering are appropriate to that era, before wartime austerity liveries became common. The signalboxes and other structures are genuine LBSCR styles, as are the superb hand-made working semaphore signal gantries (6).

In addition to electric trains, there are steam-hauled Continental expresses passing through to Newhaven Harbour, Oxted line trains to Brighton, an LMS steam service from Willesden, and various goods operations involving SR and occasionally LMS locomotives.

A few small anomalies are present, as on most layouts which are not quite complete; locomotives and other items which happen to be available for test running in the early stages of construction often survive for a long time, but eventually disappear. Some of the controls, though, with which trains are operated through East Croydon station on the multiple track main line, are the last word in accuracy. They are actual LBSCR instruments, as used in the old East Croydon signalboxes, demolished during modernisation in 1955. These together with station nameboards help to turn his 'railway room' into something of a working museum with an unusual degree of authenticity.

Whiskeyjack, near Skunk River on the CPR Mountain Subdivision (70), presents a complete

Fig 6 Ex-LBSCR H2 4-4-2 No B421 *South Foreland*, on a 'Newhaven Continental', passes main-line and suburban electric trains at East Croydon on Peter Moore's OO scale layout.

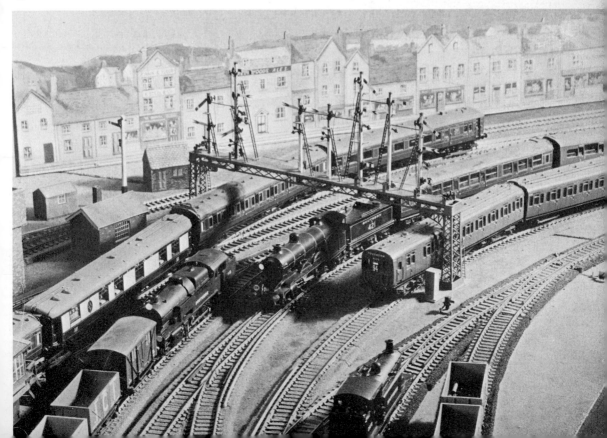

contrast to East Croydon, particularly in the extent of background scenery. Here it is no mere afterthought, filling in some odd corner of the baseboard; the railway and everything else are dominated by it. Bridges and tunnels are provided on a scale appropriate to a transcontinental prototype main line 3000 miles long, of which the 600 miles west of Calgary are mainly in alpine or sub-alpine terrain. This line traverses gorges, canyons, passes and settlements, with intriguing names like Eagle Pass, Glacier, Ottertail, Kicking Horse Canyon, the Great Divide, Medicine Hat, Moose Jaw and Thunder Bay.

The Mountain Subdivision in miniature, although as yet incomplete, is a pretty big operation with a plentiful supply of heavy motive power, of passenger and freight rolling stock; breakdown cranes, snowploughs and everything else needed to keep trains rolling in all weathers. It is not the sort of layout one can knock together in a couple of evenings; it is, however, presented as an example of scenery construction on a grand scale, to show what can be done.

Aix-Les-Bonnes (20) shows how judicious changes in buildings, signals etc can alter the apparent era or nationality of a scene; astute readers may notice similarities in background, track or turntable between this French depot

Fig 8 Landscaping with lichen (as described in Chapter Seven) calls for a delicate touch.

and the one at Skunk River in Canada (34). They are the same, but the concrete water tower is so typically French and the totally enclosed wooden one (with central heating to prevent it freezing up in winter) is so characteristic of Canada and the northern USA that little else is needed to achieve the transformation. The roundhouse and turntable are of no particular prototype but generally resemble designs found on both sides of the Atlantic. The tall 'yard lamps' are more like European than American types, but being the best ones available at the time the depot was constructed they were accepted as competent-looking models which really worked.

Foregoing examples are offered as sources of inspiration, and readers are urged not to copy closely but to analyse them and decide which features appeal to them most strongly. They may then proceed to develop their own individual styles and creative abilities, possibly assisted by a written check list of things to make, to do or to investigate further. In doing this they will need to take account of factors which will now be considered, which affect layout planning and the choice of themes for their own little railway empires.

Availability of time and space are fundamental

Fig 7 An N scale DB 'Black Forest local' with four-wheel vehicles.

factors; with time to spare you can settle down to make your own models from scratch, and with plenty of space you are not restricted in the size of layout. If, however, time is limited it is often better to build a simple layout on which commercially made locomotives and trains can run. If space is a problem, you may have to model in a small scale or adopt a small and simple layout plan; with Z gauge you can easily build a layout in a suitcase, but with gauge O or 1 a fairly large room or a garden are more suitable. Alternatively you may build a few models from scratch for exhibition or for operation on the layout of a friend or at a model railway club.

Modelling skill is another factor, but even today's most brilliant exponents of the art had to start sometime. Lack of experience should deter no-one from starting with little more than a screwdriver, a knife and a tube of glue, plus the determination to succeed.

Financial considerations may rule out the purchase of rare and expensive hand-made brass model locomotives or of the latest type of electronic controller, but for many modellers the most interesting and absorbing part of the hobby is the construction of their own models. Scratch-building calls for more skill than the assembly of commercial kits, but there is still some personal pride attached to the finishing and painting of kits. They can be ruined by sloppy painting, and they can sometimes be improved by small alterations or even transformed into a different model altogether by extensive adaptation, or 'kitbashing' (80). The layout may have to be built in instalments over a long period, allowing time for money to be saved for each new addition to the track or trains, but it might be better in any case to start with a small layout allowing possibilities for future extension.

Policies help one to make the best use of time, money, space and skill. Beginners should adopt a policy of tackling simple jobs first, before attempting to scratchbuild large and complicated locomotives or to assemble kits for working model machinery with hundreds of tiny parts. The latter sometimes give experienced modellers trouble, so it is not surprising if beginners fail to complete them!

A logical progression is from very simple plastic or printed card building kits (small houses, sheds etc) through more complex non-working kits to kits for signals and simple

Fig 9 In 1887 the Atlantic Express panted across creaking timber trestles, like this example assembled from plastic kits. (See Chapter Six for all kinds of bridges.)

vehicles. When all these come out straight, square and free from disfiguring blobs of adhesive it is time to move on to simple layout construction involving some carpentry, and to tracklaying which may involve use of a soldering iron for connecting the wiring. Cutting and bending of track, as well as nearly all soldering, may be avoided by using only the fixed formation standard track units of the mass market manufacturers of trains, designed to fit together in predetermined geometrical forms. Such firms include Hornby, Triang, Minitrix and Märklin, which provide wide ranges of standard sectional or 'snap' track and accessories suitable for building up into complete layouts. There is no quicker way of putting together a working, or even an automatically controlled model railway; but individuality and realism are reduced. Exhibition layouts for young people (11) are the real use for geometrical layouts, rather than layouts for the older and more discerning enthusiast.

With non-geometrical layouts it is best to lay one complete circle or end-to-end main line first, in order to get trains running as quickly as possible (10, 26). Branch lines, sidings, turn-tables etc can then follow at leisure. It should also be noted that level track is easier to lay than lines with gradients; it enables given locomotives to haul more, too. Bridges, tunnels and scenery often need to be planned in advance of baseboard construction but as layouts *can* be built without them it is logical to consider the various jobs to be tackled in the order of succeeding chapters devoted to specialised aspects of the hobby. In many ways these aspects are interrelated, and it is a good policy to read right through to the end before making plans or starting work.

Use of tools and materials may be learned at

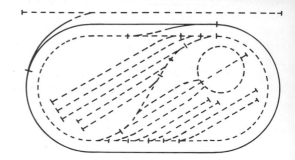

AN AMBITIOUS LAYOUT, WHERE THE SIMPLE OUTER LOOP (FULL LINE) SHOULD BE COMPLETED BEFORE LINES SHOWN DOTTED.

Fig 10

night school classes or, better still, under the personal supervision of an experienced modeller. Model railway clubs are often glad of willing help in constructing a new layout or staging an exhibition; instruction may be had in exchange for some donkey-work, and you can often observe experts in many branches of the hobby working at the same time. Clubs and exhibitions also provide opportunities to study both histori-cal and modern modelling, perhaps also North

Fig 11 Somebody's birthday? A well-designed HO scale layout using Märklin standard sectional track parts. *Märklin photo*

American, Continental European and freelance. An illustrated book may succeed in arousing interest in any or all of these aspects, but there is no real substitute for seeing and doing for yourself.

Modern modelling involves studying the present-day railway scene and reproducing a small part of it in miniature. Modern diesel and electric trains have their own appeal, while special trains run by preservation societies are often hauled by historical steam locomotives in the liveries of companies which have long ceased to exist; thus modern modellers can have the best of both worlds.

Models of contemporary trains are obtainable at most model shops while information and drawings may be found in such railway periodicals as the *Railway Magazine, Modern Railways, Railway World* (British), *Trains* (USA) or *Eisenbahn* (Continental). The most popular model railway periodicals include *Railway Modeller, Model Railway Constructor* and *Model Railways* (British); *Model Railroader* and *Railroad Model Craftsman* (USA); *Loco Revue, Rail Miniature Flash,* and *Miniaturbahnen* (Continental).

Historical modelling presents greater difficulties and therefore more of a challenge. To obtain information for example about the shapes of signals or the precise colours of locomotives and carriages in, say, 1850 or 1922 one has to visit museums, preserved lines and exhibition model railways such as the superb Midland Railway line in Derby town museum. There are the Historical Model Railway Society and societies for the study of many individual lines, such as the LMS Society, whose honorary secretaries may be reached through advertisements, club and society announcements, or a reply-paid enquiry to the editor of a railway periodical. The local model railway club may have its own library with records of local lines going back many years.

Continental European modelling involves research into the styles and methods of railway companies which are strange but still exist. Foreign travel and a knowledge of languages are essential for proper understanding, but interest in foreign trains is usually the result of travelling in them and of enjoying the sights and sounds of new lands. A good tip is to study catalogues of continental model manufacturers which are published in many languages.

North American railroading has a language which is often incomprehensible to the uninitiated, and which must be learned for proper appreciation of the finer points of modelling. Thus carriages or wagons alike are cars; a signalbox is an interlocking tower; an electric locomotive is a juice hog; an engine-driver is an engineer or hogger; a guard is a conductor, and the statement 'Towerman highballs hotshot' means 'Signalman gives clear signals to a fast freight.' So now you know! Other terms will be explained as they arise.

Firms such as Walthers in Milwaukee supply models to mail order but importers on both sides of the Atlantic handle beautiful hand finished brass Japanese and Korean models, as well as a wide range of inexpensive plastic-bodied ones. Plans and drawings are published in periodicals already mentioned, and some railway offices retail prints of workshop drawings, railway relics, timetables and photographs. Amongst these is CP Bygones at Windsor Station, Place du Canada, Montreal H3C 3E4.

Carefully prepared plans are essential for smooth and railway-like operation of a layout. They make it possible to ensure that curves on the main line will be adequate for efficient running of the largest locomotives and longest carriages, and that clearances in tunnels and under bridges will be sufficient for bulky loads or for electric locomotives with pantographs raised. They also help to avoid situations where bottlenecks in trackwork hinder busy operations, no improvement being possible without major reconstruction of baseboards and track. Nowhere is planning more necessary than in the electrical wiring and controls; more time can be spent investigating short circuits than in running trains on badly planned systems.

Individual modellers must decide their own policies regarding what to make, what to buy, which sort of layout to construct, and which company or country to adopt for their prototype. They must decide whether to adhere strictly to a particular place and time, or to mix things up and become freelance. They will then be in a position to start making detailed plans; and to assist them in this the next chapter is devoted to the scales, gauges and standards which govern the interchangeability (or otherwise) of models. These enable precise specifications to be drawn up, and clear, unambiguous descriptions to be given in succeeding chapters dealing with techniques of detailed planning, construction and operation.

CHAPTER TWO

SPECIFICATIONS

In order to specify exactly the similarities or differences between models, or between a model and a real, or prototype train, we need to establish universal standards of comparison so that all modellers, everywhere, will know what we mean. The most fundamental standards for model trains are the scale to which they are built and the gauge of the track on which they run. Both need to be specified because prototype trains run on tracks of numerous gauges; as a result there are numerous possible track gauges in each modelling scale. Table 1 lists the principal 'full size' track gauges in use; of these 4ft 8½in (1435mm) gauge is called standard gauge, while those which are smaller are called narrow gauge and those which are larger are called broad gauge.

The gauge of a track is defined as the perpendicular distance between the opposite faces of the heads of a pair of running rails, in other words the inside edge of the two rails forming a single track; dimension G in fig 12. Running rails are rails on which train wheels run; there are other rails which will be met with in Chapter Five.

Fig 12

The scale of a model is the ratio between its dimensions and those of the prototype it represents. If all dimensions are in exactly the same ratio it is a scale model; otherwise it is a hybrid or semi-scale model. However, it is unwise to be too critical as there are practical problems involved as we shall see.

Suppose we were to model a lamp, such as railwaymen might use or as might be fitted on to a train; if we made the model half the size of the prototype it would be to half scale, or 1:2. If, however, we wanted the lamp as a mere accessory

TABLE 1: PRINCIPAL PROTOTYPE TRACK GAUGES

Gauge:		Where used (example):
Narrow gauges		
mm	ft in	
600	1–11⅝	Wales (Festiniog Rly; Vale of Rheidol); Greece
686	2–3	Wales (Tal y Llyn Rly)
750	2–5½	Germany; Egypt; Indonesia
760	2–6	Wales (Welshpool & Llanfair); Austria (Zillertalbahn); India
800	2–7½	Wales (Snowdon Mountain Rly); Switzerland (Wengernalp Railway)
914	3–0	Isle of Man; Ireland (County Donegal); USA (D & RGW); Canada (WP & Y)
950	3–1½	Italy (Dolomites Rly; Sardinia)
*1000	3–3⅜	Germany; Switzerland (secondary lines); Spain; India Greece etc; East Africa (Kenya, Uganda, Tanzania)
*1067	3–6	Australia (Western); South Africa; Japan; Spain; East Africa (Rhodesia, Zambia, Mozambique); Canada (CNR Newfoundland)
Standard gauge		
1435	4–8½	(worldwide)
Broad gauges		
1524	5–0	USSR; Finland
1600	5–3	Ireland (CIE; GNR; NCC); Australia
1676	5–6	Spain; India
2140	7–0¼	Britain (GWR broad gauge until 1892)

Note: very small differences (eg between 1674 and 1676mm gauges) have been ignored. For exact dimensions, see *World Railways* (Sampson Low) or other reference works.
*1 metre or 3ft 6in gauges as applicable are the principal main line gauges in South and East Africa, Japan, Western Australia and parts of India and in terms of locomotive size and power are the equal of many standard gauge lines.

to fit on to a model train (and not as a table ornament) a scale of 1:2 would be far too big. We might have modelled a train to scales of 1:10, 1:50 or 1:100; and the results of so doing are tabulated in fig 13, below. The dimension given in each case is the overall height, over the raised handle. In fig 13A is a front view of the

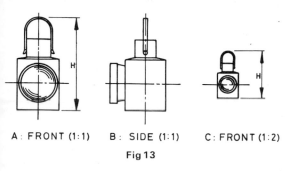

A: FRONT (1:1)   B: SIDE (1:1)   C: FRONT (1:2)

Fig 13

Scale:	1:1	1:2	1:10	1:50	1:100
H; in	10	5	1	0·2	0·1
H; mm	254	127	25·4	5·1	2·5

Note: There are 25·4mm to 1in; figures involving amounts less than 0·1mm have been rounded off as they are outside the degree of accuracy to which most modellers work.

prototype, drawn to a scale of one tenth or 1:10; in fig 13B is the corresponding side view and in fig 13C is a front view of a 1:2 scale model also drawn to 1:10 scale. The tabulation, using letter H for the overall height, avoids the need for drawing each size of model in turn; this is a method adopted frequently in this book. The terms front and side elevations (instead of views) will also be adopted where appropriate.

In fig 1 we can compare the front elevations of typical British, North American and Continental European steam locomotives all drawn to the same scale of 1:76 or approximately 4mm to 1ft. The difference in size between LNER P2 class

2-8-2 No 2001 *Cock O' The North* (fig 1A) and CPR T-1-b class semi-streamlined Selkirk 2-10-4 No 5928 (fig 1B) is sufficient to cause problems with clearances in tunnels, under bridges and through stations with raised platforms, if No 5928 were to be run on an LNER layout. A glance at fig 14 shows there is also a problem with length, causing difficulties on turntables and on curves where the large rear overhang will cause the back of the cab to create havoc amongst lineside objects or passing trains.

If, however, No 5928 were redrawn to 3.5mm/ft, or HO scale, it would appear only slightly larger than *Cock O' The North*, and some of the problems of running North American models on British layouts are usually solved in this way. The SNCF American-built 141R 2-8-2 (fig 1C) is of intermediate height and width, appearing slightly smaller than *Cock O' The North* when reduced to HO scale.

There are, or were, locomotives on the NP and certain other US lines 17ft tall, and many Russian and East European types were lofty too, but they are less typical than the examples illustrated.

Some modellers like all their equipment to be strictly to scale; and all to the same scale at that! To help modellers who wish to be careful about scales, Table 2 lists principal model railway scales and gauges. Some of these are very popular and some are not common nowadays; but all might be found when dealing with second-hand models or collectors' items. The normal small scale popular commercial gauges are shown in bold.

Fig 14 Side elevations of LNER P2 2-8-2 and CPR T-1-b 2-10-4 drawn to the same scale. **FO** front overhang. **RW** rigid wheelbase. **RO** rear overhang.

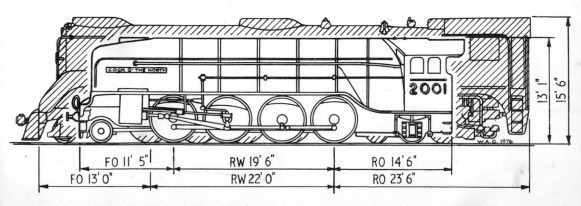

TABLE 2: PRINCIPAL MODEL RAILWAY SCALES & GAUGES

Scale	Ratio	mm/ft	in/ft	Gauge mm	in	Concise code	Notes
Z	1 : 220	1·4		6		220(Z)6	
N	1 : 160	1·9		9		160(N)9	
N(B)	1 : 148	2·1		9		148(N)9	
OOO	1 : 152	2		9·5		152(N)9·5	1
TT	1 : 120	2·5		12		120(TT)12	
TT(B)	1 : 102	3		12		102(TT)12	2
TT(C)	1 : 100	3		13		100(TT)13	3
HO(C)	1 : 90	3·4		16·5		90(HO)16·5	4
HO	1 : 87·1	3·5		16·5		87(HO)16·5	
HO(C)	1 : 85	3·6		16·5		85(HO)16·5	5
HO(C)	1 : 82	3·7		16·5		82(HO)16·5	6
OO(B)	1 : 76·2	4		16·5		76(OO)16·5	
EM(B)	1 : 76·2	4		18		76(EM)18	
P4(B)	1 : 76·2	4		18·8		76(P4)18·8	7
OO(A)	1 : 76·2	4		19		76(OO)19	
S	1 : 64	4·8	$\frac{3}{16}$	22·2	$\frac{7}{8}$	64(S)22·2	
Q(A)	1 : 48	6·4	$\frac{1}{4}$	30·2	$1\frac{3}{16}$	48(Q)30·2	
O(A)	1 : 48	6·4	$\frac{1}{4}$	31·7	$1\frac{1}{4}$	48(O)31·7	
O(C)	1 : 45	6·8		32		45(O)32	8
O17(A)	1 : 45	6·8	$\frac{17}{64}$	31·7	$1\frac{1}{4}$	45(O)31·7	
O	1 : 43·5	7		32		43·5(O)32	8
1(A)	1 : 32	9·5	$\frac{3}{8}$	44·5	$1\frac{3}{4}$	32(1)44·5	
1(C)	1 : 32	9·5		45		32(1)45	
1(B)	1 : 30·5	10		45		30·5(1)45	

All the above refer to models of standard gauge railways. (A) means North America; (B) Britain; (C) Continental Europe.

Notes:
1. Has largely been supplanted by N
2. Also known as TT3
3. Used by Swiss firm of Wesa
4. Was used by Trix Express in 1960s
5. Used by Fleischmann for European models
6. Was used by Fleischmann and Rivarossi in 1960s
7. Also called Protofour
8. 1 : 45 is a standard scale on the Continent but 1 : 43·5 is also used in France, as well as in Britain.

The briefest glance shows that OO/HO represents not one but a whole family of scales, of which only HO with a ratio of 1:87.1 is strictly correct for 16.5mm track gauge; all other scales using this gauge are hybrids. The most frequent reason for the development of hybrid scales such as OO, which arose 40 and more years ago, has been the restricted space between the frames and the outside limits of locomotives built to the British loading gauge, for there is often insufficient space to fit robust wheels and motion with the clearances necessary for reliable operation. In the past there was little clearance to fit the then available electric motors inside the bodies of 1:87 British locomotive models. Larger scales than those appropriate to the track gauge, in the ratio 1:76, were therefore adopted for the bodies. The compromises resulting from this practice have produced the very popular OO scale, amongst others, which is too well established to give way completely to a pure scale for a long time to come.

There are, however, several alternative scales and gauges available to the purist who wishes to model British trains accurately, while still enjoying the advantages of being able to use many commercially available components. The modeller wanting a correctly scaled layout should select one track gauge or scale ratio as the datum point, and derive all other dimensions from it. Starting with a ratio of 1:76 the track gauge is derived as 1435/76, or 18.9mm. Starting with 4mm to 1ft gives the same result (rounding off decimal points less than 0.1mm) so it comes as no surprise to find North American OO and the British P4 or Protofour in close agreement here.

Where North American OO and British

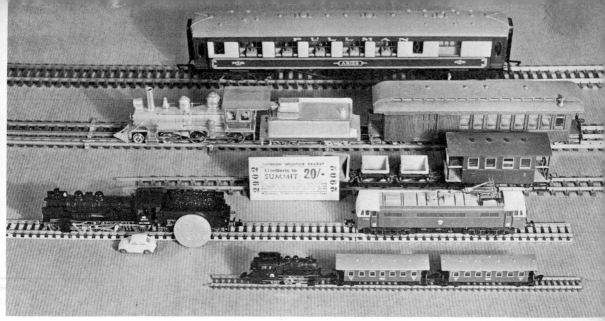

Fig 15 *(Front to rear):* Front track: Märklin 220(Z)6 train. Second track: Fleischmann 160(N)9 DB 4-6-0 with VW 'beetle' car and 5p coin; Lima 148(N)9 BR electric loco. Third track: 87(HOn)9 tip-wagons and coach. Fourth track: FED Spartan 87(HOn)10.5 brass Baldwin 4-4-0 and Tomalco 87(HOn)10.5 wood combine (ie coach/baggage car). Fifth track: Hornby 76(OO)16.5 Pullman parlour car *Aries.*

Protofour modelling differ is in the choice of standards for wheels and axles; the former is associated with NMRA standard profiles and the latter has a unique set of its own. In Chapter Five reference is made to wheel, axle and rail profiles; at this stage we can note that they exist, and leave them for future consideration. Continental European standards are set by MOROP, who publish standards called NEM (in several different languages), while in Britain the BRMSB has attempted to obtain a degree of standardisation.

Another of the OO/HO family is EM scale, meaning eighteen millimetre and using 18mm track gauge. This is still a compromise but enables some commercial OO models to be adapted quite easily, while still leaving a little extra clearance between locomotive frames and outside limits. Like P4, though, it is a scale for enthusiasts who are prepared to make or adapt most of their equipment; commercial support is very thin.

A concise code has been introduced into Table 2 to permit us to describe clearly and un-ambiguously the scale and gauge of models referred to in subsequent illustrations and text. It is not intended to replace existing names of well-known scales, but it does provide distinc-tions between eight members of the OO/HO family, four varieties of gauge O and three each for gauge 1 and TT.

Z scale is the smallest scale for commercial models (15 and 16) at time of writing (1977). It has the advantage of requiring the least space for a given layout plan; and if the layout must be confined to a small suitcase this is the right scale to adopt! Building models from scratch and carrying out repairs and maintenance are jobs for watchmakers and instrument engineers, though.

N scale has grown rapidly in popularity in the 1970s and it enjoys large-scale commercial support. Scratchbuilding one's own models is possible, but hardly necessary with so much equipment already available and the painting and lettering of trains in this scale is decidedly tricky.

OOO or treble-O scale was introduced by Lone Star more as a toyshop product than one for modelling; it is kept alive by modellers in 2mm/1ft scale even though N scale has captured the mass market. Little commercial support remains.

TT scale has also largely been supplanted by N scale, leaving modellers in 3mm/1ft scale with little commercial support. In the early 1960s it was quite popular and second-hand models produced by Triang are often still obtainable.

OO and HO scales are the international favourites, for models of this size are small enough for a fair-sized layout to be fitted into a modern house and yet large enough to be quite robust, repairable and suitable for scratchbuild-ing, painting and lettering.

S scale is adopted by scratchbuilders who find OO or HO a little too small for them. Machining of parts, rivet embossing and other detailing operations are somewhat easier in S scale, but there is little or no commercial support.

O, O17 and Q scales are ideal for old houses, barns, gardens or clubs with plenty of space to work in. Scratchbuilding is a simple matter and painting and lettering are much less finicky than in OO or HO. Commercial support tends to be with cheap plastic equipment suitable for use by children, or with metal wheels, castings and other parts suitable for the scratchbuilder or assembler of kits. Fully assembled scale models in gauge O tend to be rather expensive. 'Coarse scale' gauge O uses crudely oversized wheel treads and flanges suited to early tinplate track; the alternative is called 'fine scale' but some manufacturers have an in-between compromise.

Gauge 1 is generally considered to be the largest size (it is never, for some reason, called scale 1) in railway modelling; anything bigger comes under the heading of model engineering, and is better suited to live steam locomotives hauling a train of live passengers round an outdoor track.

So far, we have considered scales and gauges for modelling prototype standard gauge trains, but they occupy only one line in Table 1!

Broad-gauge modelling is restricted to individuals who follow Irish practice and to commercial suppliers of kits for nineteenth-century GWR

equipment, but narrow-gauge modelling is well established and has commercial support. Early commercial models were of metre-gauge trains by Zeuke of East Germany and of contractors' railways or the very lightest of public railway equipment by Eggerbahn (87). Then came the superb range of Zillertalbahn and other Austrian equipment by Liliput, while British firms produced kits for modelling the justly famous preserved lines in Wales. By 1970 it was a poor exhibition that lacked a narrow-gauge layout or two, and many a standard-gauge layout featured a working, abandoned or preserved narrow-gauge line.

Scales and gauges for narrow-gauge lines may be established by taking the ratio, such as 1:76, and the prototype gauge, such as 686mm which is that of the Talyllyn Railway; then the model narrow gauge is 686/76 or 9mm, near enough. This means that N scale track and mechanisms may be used as a starting point for modelling the Talyllyn particularly if it is part of an OO scale model with standard gauge trains, and the only glaring error will be in the size and spacing of sleepers, or cross-ties. These may either be replaced or simply hidden under simulated ashes, weeds etc. Other convenient adaptations for metre-gauge in HO on TT track, and in TT on N track and in N on Z track are given in Table 3 below.

It will be seen that some of the resulting model narrow gauges do not quite fit any popular prototype; but this is unlikely to deter narrow-gauge enthusiasts from using artists' licence and adopting 455 or 520 instead of 600mm as a prototype gauge. Kits for both Talyllyn (686mm) and Festiniog (600mm) trains were introduced by GEM (Britain) using 12mm gauge track which

Fig 16 *(Front to rear):* Front track: Hornby gauge O tinplate flat wagon. Second track: 5p coin inside 148(N)9 wagon in 76(OO)16·5 wagon plus 43·5(O)32 wagon in 32(1)45 wagon. Third track: 220(Z)6 train plus 148(N)9 train plus 76(OO)16·5 0-6-0T on 22(G)45 flat wagon; LGB22(G) 45 'hood' diesel locomotive.

TABLE 3: MODEL NARROW GAUGES

Name	Scale ratio	mm/ft	in/ft	Gauge mm	Equivalent prototype Gauge; mm	Concise code	Notes
N–6	1:160	1·9		6	960	160(Nn)6	1,7
N–6(B)	1:148	2·1		6	888	148(Nn)6	1
HO–6	1:87	3·5		6	520	87(HOn)6	1
OO–6	1:76	4		6	455	76(OOn)6	1
TTn3(B)	1:102	3		9	914	102(TTn)9	2,10
HO–9	1:87	3·5		9	780	87(HOn)9	2,8
OO–9	1:76	4		9	686	76(OOn)9	2,9
HOn3(A)	1:87	3.5		10·5	914	87(HOn)10·5	3,10
HO–12	1:87	3·5		12	1000	87(HOn)12	4,7
OOn3(B)	1:76	4		12	914	76(OOn)12	4,10
(B)	1:56	5·5		12	673	56(n)12	4
On3(A)	1:48	6·4	$\frac{1}{4}$	19	914	48(On)19	5,10
G(C)	1:22	14		45	990	22(G)45	6,7

(A) means North America; (B) Britain; (C) Continental Europe

Notes:
1. Z scale mechanisms may be used
2. N scale mechanisms may be used
3. a standard North American modelling gauge
4. TT scale mechanisms may be used
5. some models available in North America
6. popular LGB garden railway; will run on gauge 1 track
7. for modelling metre-gauge prototypes
8. for modelling 750 and 760mm gauge prototypes
9. for modelling 2ft 3in gauge prototypes
10. for modelling 3ft gauge prototypes

makes a common prototype 673mm, a fair compromise. North American narrow-gauge modelling, with its commercial support, seems to centre around the DRGW 3ft gauge, while Continental metre-gauge trains in the large G scale (narrow gauge types on 45mm track) are well provided for by LGB of West Germany (16).

Choosing the right scale and gauge for your layout and trains is an exercise depending upon the available space and upon the extent to which you are prepared to make your own track and other equipment from scratch. If you are able to make all necessary parts, then any scale may be chosen; if commercially available track and other equipment is to be used it is necessary to settle on one of the established scales and gauges already described. If you want to operate very long trains (passenger trains of 10 or more vehicles, or freight trains of 30 or more wagons) but have very limited space in which to build a layout, you either have to adopt a small scale (eg Z, N or possibly OO or HO) or to join a

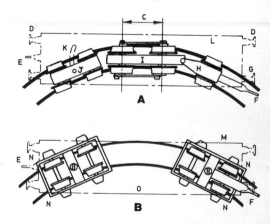

Fig 18 Problems caused by fouling of buffers by couplings on locomotive A and coach B on tight curves are self-evident.

club where facilities for long trains are freely available.

Curves and clearances need to have more generous proportions if locomotives with large rigid wheelbases or passenger vehicles with long bodies and large overhangs are to be used (see 17 and 18). Shorter locomotives and some articulated locomotives, short passenger and freight vehicles will all run on layouts having tighter clearances and shorter radius curves. The ugly gap between long coaches is unrealistic; the shorter coaches look much happier, even on a tighter curve. The answer is obvious: stick to short vehicles, use wider radius curves or adopt a smaller scale altogether. It might well be a case of back to the drawing board!

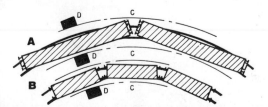

Fig 17 Short coaches B need less clearance than long ones A; obstructions D must be outside clearance lines C.

Fig 19 Massive CPR Selkirk 2-10-4s and *(right)* a UP Big Boy 4-8-8-4 (World's largest steam locomotive type) look natural on gentle mainline curves. Note caboose and tight curves *(left)*.

Fig 20 A Jouef 87(HO)16.5 SNCF 241P 4-8-2 rides the turntable at Aix-Les-Bonnes. Note the wine-barrel wagon and 16-wheel low-loader wagon carrying a generator *(right)*.

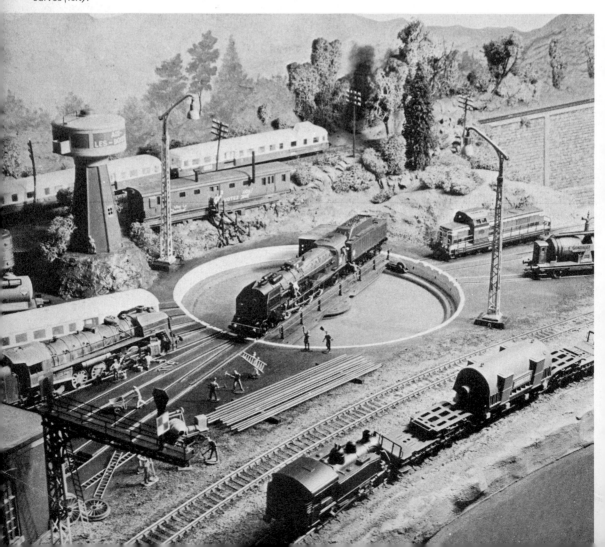

CHAPTER THREE

AT THE DRAWING BOARD

Professional drawing office staff not only have their drawing boards, tee-squares, set-squares and drawing instruments but also scale rules, conversion tables and outlines of standard components which they use for numerous projects. Railway modellers, too, can benefit by adopting similar aids.

Scales we have already covered, but if we wish to construct a model for gauge O, for instance, and the only available plans are drawn to OO scale, we require a rapid and certain method of converting dimensions (see Appendix 1).

Standard components which we may wish to use over and over again are layout elements such as straight and curved tracks, turnouts, turntables, platforms etc and these must be considered in relation to train lengths and clearances. They are specified here not only in terms of scale and gauge but also according to whether they are for use on a main or a branch line; or an industrial, narrow gauge or con-tractor's line. The latter are considered to be the most diminutive, using a track gauge of around 2ft or 2ft 6in (for prototype track) and extremely tight curves.

Arbitrary minimum radii for curves are assigned in fig 23 for OO or HO scales which, with reasonable care in construction and opera-tion, will allow smooth and realistic train movements with vehicles of all but the most abnormal dimensions. From these radii and from other factors such as widths of models, overhang on curves and minimum widths of station platforms we are able to build up a set of figures indicating how much space we must allow for a wide range of layout elements. Using these as a guide, we can quickly and confidently put together plans for all kinds of layouts without having to worry too much about possible snags due to inadequate clearances.

These figures are, however, no more than a guide. One may increase train lengths and plat-form widths etc to any desired degree, while the only really certain way to determine accurately all necessary clearances is to buy or borrow the longest and widest vehicle ever likely to run on the projected new layout and to check it on straight and curved tracks with a cardboard

Fig 21 Curves are sharp on narrow-gauge lines, as on BR's Vale of Rheidol tracks at Devil's Bridge terminus. *T. J. Edgington*

tunnel mouth and station platform.

Not everyone will wish to model in OO or HO scales, of course, and corresponding figures for other scales and gauges may be obtained by use of fig 146 in Appendix 1 (page 88).

Layout elements are shown diagrammatically (with a single thick line for each track) in figs 22 and 23 for those who wish to design their own layouts. The alternative is to copy layout plans published in periodicals or in the catalogues and planbooks of the larger manufacturers. The latter are designed around standard sizes of sectional track, turnouts, crossings, etc, for those who like their trackwork to come ready made; and layouts designed in this way tend to resemble geometric figures. With the use of standard sectional track parts there is no allow-ance for transition curves, which permit trains

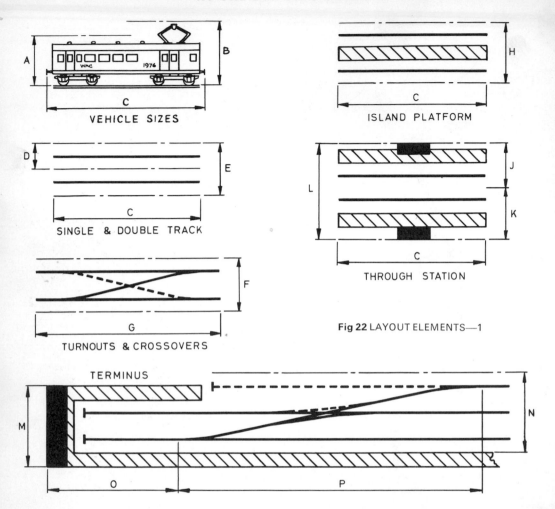

VEHICLE SIZES

ISLAND PLATFORM

SINGLE & DOUBLE TRACK

THROUGH STATION

TURNOUTS & CROSSOVERS

Fig 22 LAYOUT ELEMENTS—1

TERMINUS

		British		N A	Cont
		OO	HO	HO	HO
Scale, mm/1ft:		4	3·5	3·5	3·5
A minimum	mm	52	48	60	56
maximum	mm	56	50	66	62
B minimum	mm	68	60	75	68
maximum	mm	80	70	90	84
C short	mm	140	123	220	160
medium	mm	240	210	270	270
long	mm	270	236	300	320
D	mm	45	40	45	42
E	mm	95	83	95	91
F	mm	100	88	100	96
G	mm	500	450	500	480
H	mm	140	123	120	116
J	mm	90	79	80	78
K	mm	120	104	120	118
L	mm	210	184	200	196
M	mm	175	153	160	156
N	mm	150	132	150	144
O	mm	315	280	385	350
P short	mm	450	410	450	435
medium	mm	650	580	650	630
long	mm	850	770	850	825

to move from straight to curved track or vice versa in a smooth and railway-like manner; this is an inherent fault which is often noticeable at exhibitions.

Vehicle sizes are a good starting point for establishing a set of standard components, and in fig 22 A, B, and C we give overhead clearances with and without pantographs as well as length over buffers (or over couplers) for a range of vehicles, and for two scales. As a rough guide, 1.9mm/1ft scale (N gauge) sizes are just over half those for 3.5mm/1ft, or just less than half those of 4mm/1ft scale, while 7mm/1ft scale sizes are exactly double 3.5mm/1ft scale.

These dimensions given are not exact loading gauge dimensions which vary from railway to railway (fig 1) but clearances which should be allowed to permit passage of all normal vehicles. Height clearances in fig 22A are minimum for normal lines; maximum for lines having very

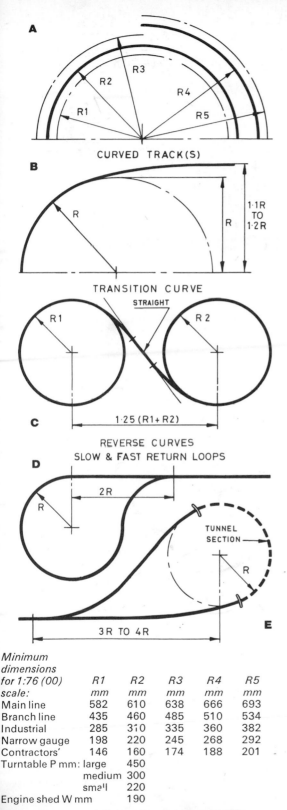

A

R3
R2
R4
R1
R5

CURVED TRACK(S)

B

R
R
1·1R
TO
1·2R

TRANSITION CURVE

STRAIGHT
R1
R2

C

1·25 (R1+R2)

REVERSE CURVES
SLOW & FAST RETURN LOOPS

D

2R
R

TUNNEL
SECTION
R

3R TO 4R

E

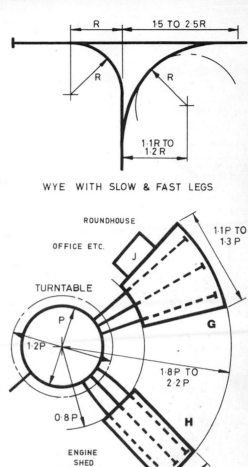

R   1·5 TO 2·5R
R   R
1·1R TO
1·2 R

WYE WITH SLOW & FAST LEGS

ROUNDHOUSE
OFFICE ETC.
J
1·1P TO
1·3 P
TURNTABLE
P
1·2P
G
1·8P TO
2·2 P
0·8P
H
ENGINE
SHED
W
WAC
1976

Fig 23 LAYOUT ELEMENTS—2

high tunnels, overbridges, etc. Some pantographs or trolleys can safely be depressed almost to roof level in tunnels and under bridges, but other types click into the closed position (where they stay!) and it is wise to be fairly generous with space.

Lengths of passenger vehicles vary considerably and fig 22C gives a choice of three sizes corresponding to 4- or 6-wheelers of the early 1900s; shorter types of 8-wheelers; and the longest types in general use. Dimension C, in all its varieties, is used as the basis for minimum lengths of sidings and platforms; to allow for a 3-coach train the required length is $3 \times C$ plus a small allowance for coupling slack and for buffer stops or bumpers at the end of the siding.

Dimension D gives clearance to be allowed across the width of the coach; no wall, signal or

Minimum dimensions for 1:76 (00) scale:	R1 mm	R2 mm	R3 mm	R4 mm	R5 mm
Main line	582	610	638	666	693
Branch line	435	460	485	510	534
Industrial	285	310	335	360	382
Narrow gauge	198	220	245	268	292
Contractors'	146	160	174	188	201
Turntable P mm: large	450				
medium	300				
small	220				
Engine shed W mm	190				

other obstruction should approach closer than the chain-dotted lines.

Double track on main running lines requires a clearance shown in fig 22E, and on lines in yards and at important stations by fig 22F; the latter leaves room for railway staff to work in the space between stationary trains.

Turnouts, single and double crossovers and slips (see Chapter Five for descriptions of all types of trackwork) fit more easily into clearance fig 22F; they will go into clearance E but difficulties in accommodating electric operating mechanisms, etc, are greatly increased. If in doubt, be generous. Similarly with G, where lack of space can ruin the arrangement and lead to badly cramped track parts with consequent rough running, sparking and derailments.

Island platform clearance fig 22H is just sufficient for passengers to alight but not if there is a footbridge or shelter; these are assumed to be placed at the *end* of the platform.

Through station clearances fig 22J, K and L allow for a small shelter and station house; a footbridge could also be fitted in. Sometimes there is a fence or narrow walkway between the tracks (mainly on the Continent) or even a middle platform for parcels traffic or transfer passengers. Extra space is required for these features.

Terminus clearances fig 22M, N, O and P allow for one medium length coach in the short platform track and for the uncoupling and escape of a medium length locomotive from the long platform. Do not forget to allow for overhang of the platform by the front end of say a 4-6-0 or 4-6-2 locomotive escaping over the crossover. Width allows for the closest possible tracks and the narrowest platforms with no footbridge or shelters; the station house goes at the end beyond the buffer stops or bumpers. If space permits, it could go equally well alongside the end of either platform, logically the longer of the two as this would handle principal traffic while the shorter one would have only a railcar, parcels van or spare coach.

Minimum radii of curves for single and double track; for main, branch, industrial, narrow gauge and contractors' lines are given in fig 23A and adjacent table, together with clearances. No obstruction of any kind should appear inside the chain-dotted lines.

Transition curves (described in Chapter Five) require the centreline of straight track to be moved out to an arbitrary distance of about 1.2R and linked by a curve with a radius becoming larger as it meets the straight.

Reverse curves provide a very satisfying spectacle as a long train snakes over them, provided that they have the proper transition curves. There should be a fairly straight and level one-coach-long section in the middle, otherwise very long vehicles might be restrained by couplings from negotiating the sudden reversal of the curve particularly if curves are sharp and end overhang of the coaches too great. On a slow-speed or industrial branch line there will probably be no transition curves but at least the allowance shown in fig 23C should be made on all fast main lines. Moreover on full size lines, curved track will be banked (called cant, or in model parlance, superelevation) so that the outside rail is higher than the inner. In smaller scales this is unnecessary, although some modellers build their main lines with some superelevation and done well it can look very effective. However, it needs precise work and gradual run out at the end of a curve otherwise it can make rolling stock unstable. Beginners should avoid it.

Return loops with and without transition curves are shown in fig 23D and E; in real life these had their uses for turning round whole trains at North American termini, which had baggage cars at the front and, often, special observation cars at the tail. A turntable and roundhouse frequently occupied the space inside the loop. A switcher (shunting locomotive) coupled up to the rear of a newly arrived train and hauled it in reverse around the return loop surrounding the roundhouse. It was then facing the right direction for its next trip, after cleaning. Note that loop fig 23E takes up more space than D but its smooth transition curves make it very suitable for hiding the circular curve out of sight in a tunnel. D is for very slow train movements while E can be taken at full speed.

Wyes (triangles) are another North American feature enabling locomotives to be turned without the expense of a turntable. Fig 23F shows a wye having transition curves on the right-hand leg only; this would be part of a fast main line while the other two legs would be used for turning locomotives.

Turntables and roundhouses occupy a fair amount of space, as fig 23G and H shows. Clearance around the turntable is essential in case locomotive buffers, couplings etc project beyond the edge of the table itself. Lines are so close together at the edge of the turntable that locomotives cannot stand on adjacent tracks; in order to allow them to stand in a row, clear of the roundhouse building, the radius to the entrance must be increased from the suggested minimum of 0.8P up to at least 1.5P, with corresponding increases in the other radii. The latter can vary according to whether or not the house has buffer stops or bumpers inside, or arrangements of levers which automatically close the doors behind the locomotive as it enters. It is assumed that no locomotive over buffers or couplers greatly exceeds in length the turntable diameter; if it does it will be difficult to position for turning and its length may prevent the doors (if fitted) from closing.

Engine sheds of the straight-sided type, shown in fig 23H, are narrower but the same considerations regarding length apply. Also, the curved tracks should not be too cramped or locomotives may jerk and derail on entering or leaving the turntable.

Store sheds or offices, fig 23J, are necessary parts of any motive power depot, and these should be included somewhere against the roundhouse or engine shed wall. Large installations also have workshops, boiler houses, sandhouses etc.

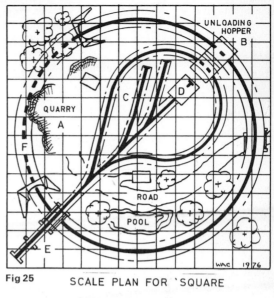

Fig 25   SCALE PLAN FOR 'SQUARE CIRCLE QUARRY' LAYOUT

Circles of track (fig 24A) may not appear to offer much scope for interesting layouts, but with a narrow gauge contractor's system (B) superimposed at a higher level (fig 25) things look altogether different. At quarry fig 25A the mechanical excavator loads rock into 87 (HO) 9mm or 76 (OO) 9mm tip wagons, which are hauled round to the unloader fig 25B; a trip wire may be arranged to tip the wagon bodies, discharging real or imitation rock into 76 (OO) 16.5mm wagons on the track below. At sidings fig 25C, spare wagons or another short train may be stored, while engines are housed in a shed D. The unloaded contractor's train runs round the rest of the loop over trestle E, which serves as a headshunt for drawing out trains before reversing them into sidings or around the loop. Meanwhile, the lower train may hide in tunnel F or even be unloaded into a box under the baseboard by hand or by some automatic unloading device.

When drawing such a layout to scale, one marks off drawing paper into convenient squares (eg 1 square equals 2 inches) and layout elements are drawn on, complete with clearance lines where appropriate. If desired, separate assemblies such as the upper level contractor's line may be drawn separately and transferred to the main layout plan with tracing or carbon paper. Finally, a small sketch makes it easier to visualise the finished layout, which we will call Square Circle Quarry.

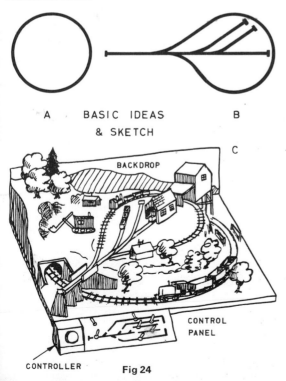

A   BASIC IDEAS & SKETCH   B

C

BACKDROP

CONTROL PANEL

CONTROLLER   **Fig 24**

End-to-end running makes work for the operating staff but for that reason alone it is more interesting than incessant circular motion.

Fig 26

The basic idea is shown in fig 26, where A is a short platform suitable for one railcar or a locomotive pulling or pushing one driving trailer or autocoach, to which it is permanently attached while on the line (31,136). This may run through C (a short tunnel, a partition wall or even a stretch or track with any desired number of curves or wayside stations) to station B, which might have platforms for two such railcars or auto trains. The operator at A may not know which of them to expect on the next scheduled arrival; there is an element of variety. The basic scheme can be enlarged to the limit of your space until there are say 20 platforms at each terminal station and six running tracks in between, if desired!

Engine changing facilities add interest, as in fig 27. Suppose a train has arrived at station A;

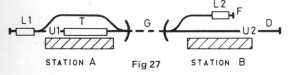

Fig 27

engine L1 is uncoupled (by hand or by mechanical or electrical uncoupling device, U1) and it runs into the headshunt then round into tunnel (or track) G. It then reverses to couple on to the other end of the train, which it pulls to station B. Here it is uncoupled and runs forward to position D. A second engine L2 now moves from its siding into position G, reverses on to the train and pulls it back to A. The engine left behind at D runs light through station B to G and reverses to siding F. We are now back to where we started, except that the engines have changed positions. Again, this may be elaborated

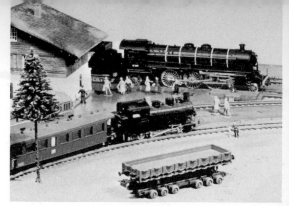

Fig 29 A Zeuke 87(HOn)12 train meets a Trix ExpressDB main-line 18[6] 4-6-2 at Unterwald on a 1959 portable layout. *W. A. Corkill.*

to any extent, using many tracks, lengthy trains and a large collection of locomotives.

Llantaffy Wells layout plan (fig 28) is drawn to scale but with the clearance lines omitted for clarity. Basically this is fig 27B with additional sidings; engines may uncouple at U1 and run round the train ready to return to another station (off the plan to the left, somewhere). If there is another railcar or train standing at platform 2, the engine can uncouple at U1 and move forward on to the level crossing while another engine leaves the shed via the double slip and the headshunt, for the return journey. If it is a goods train it may now reverse over the double slip to pick up or set down wagons at the goods shed; or wagons of locomotive coal may be set down at U4 ready for pushing forward to the coaling platform by an engine waiting at the far end of the headshunt HS. Two signal boxes are shown, but only one is needed. If the line over the level crossing continued to another station a box could be placed as shown, handy for operating the crossing gates; if, however, the line ends there the logical place for a box is at the *other* end of the station, next to signal S1, and of course the level crossing would not be needed if the road could pass round the end of the track.

The dotted extension may be used for an extra coach or parcels van, or for changing engines at platform 2 while platform 1 is occupied. An extra uncoupling device would be needed under the footbridge for engine-changing. This is a compact example of a station layout with numerous interesting possibilities.

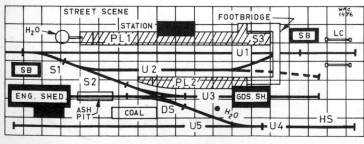

Fig 28

Shuntingdon Central (fig 30) is a terminus with a traverser attached in order to keep it supplied with trains to and from some distant destination. Main line trains normally arrive on the down main line, crossing over to platform 1 if they are too long for platform 2. Engines uncoupling at U4 may escape over the crossover (shown dotted) or wait until another engine from the sheds draws the train away. If engines are plentiful, the cost and complication of the crossover between platform ends may be dispensed

is possible to operate the main line with platform 2 and the branch line with platform 1 simultaneously. Suppose it was required to shunt empty coaches from platform 1 alongside the cattle pen; the most convenient way would be to move the coaches forward onto the branch, wait until main line trains had arrived or departed at platforms 1 and 2, and then shunt over DS1, DS2 and U2. Alternatively, headshunt HS1 (dotted) could be used; this would leave the branch line free and by means of a crossover (dotted) from down to up main lines a lengthy main line train could enter platform 1. The more alternative paths there are, the greater the operational flexibility but the greater the cost. The least expensive way to get this layout started with some real operational possibilities is to put in DS1, DS2, U3 and the traverser.

The traverser is just a board sliding on smooth metal or hard plastic strips (shown black). It may be locked in position by inserting a nail in a tight

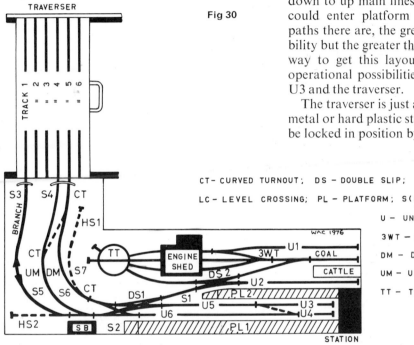

Fig 30

LAYOUT DIAGRAM FOR SHUNTINGDON CENTRAL

CT- CURVED TURNOUT; DS – DOUBLE SLIP; HS- HEADSHUNT

LC- LEVEL CROSSING; PL – PLATFORM; S(B) – SIGNAL (BOX)

U – UNCOUPLING DEVICE

3WT – 3 WAY TURNOUT

DM – DOWN MAIN LINE

UM – UP MAIN LINE

TT – TURNTABLE

with; with a three-road engine shed there should be no shortage of motive power! The shed is so arranged that engines may leave either end of it and the operational flexibility of it is almost perfect. Failure of double slip DS2 *could* stop all movements between station and shed so some alternative route to and from the turntable would be an advantage if the layout were to be used at a busy exhibition or club. Readers may like to find their own solutions to this problem.

There is a path from each platform to each main line and branch line track; furthermore, it

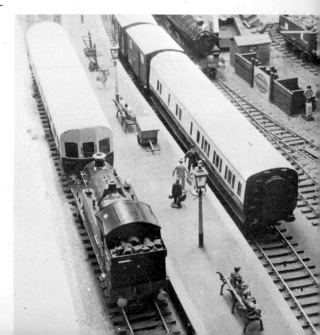

Fig 31 A 43·5(O)32 GWR '4500' 2-6-2T coupled to an auto-trailer coach for branch-line 'push-pull' service at Knoll's Green. (See fig 136.) Note the single brake-third coach *(right)*, and contact studs between the rails.

fitting hole while trains are moving on and off, and electrical connection to each track in use may be made by strips of spring brass or bronze or, better still, by flexible electrical wiring to each individual traverser track. Each track (or half of it, to allow for storage of *two* short trains) then requires its own separate isolating switch on a nearby control panel. Suppose, in the position shown, a branch line train enters traverser track 1. Assuming there is no turning loop on the other side of the traverser, it will be necessary to re-move the engine by hand and to couple it to the Shuntingdon end of the train. Now it is ready for the eventual return journey.

The traverser is moved to the right until track 2 is aligned with the down main line; an express leaves track 2 and enters platform 1. The traverser now moves back to the position shown, and the branch line train returns to platform 2; it could just as easily have returned on the down main line, with the traverser moved completely over to the right. And so on. At exhibitions the traver-ser or fiddle yard (a set of sidings where trains can be remarshalled, by hand if necessary) is usually hidden behind a tunnel under some scenery, or at least by a screen so that viewers can imagine that trains really are coming and going some distance.

Continuous running requires a circle or loop somewhere on the layout, and this is most useful to keep things going while to and fro operations are held up by some breakdown. Forgetting the four main tracks and the numerous platforms, Peter Moore's East Croydon (figs 6, 32) reduces essentially to an oval with passing loops and a branch terminus at Selhurst. The real Selhurst is a through station, but a terminus suited the desired operating pattern and a bit of artists' licence was used. So were gradients to enable the

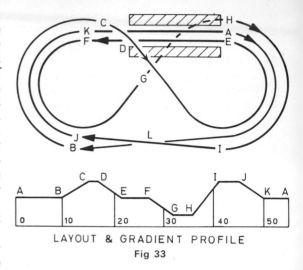

LAYOUT & GRADIENT PROFILE

Fig 33

main oval to run underneath Selhurst station, not more than about 1 in 60, but enough to mean setting out baseboard and track levels with a depth gauge as well as a spirit level.

The Tramworth or 'over and under' layout (fig 33) is nothing more than a single, continuous oval of track, so twisted that trains eventually pass through the station in *both* directions. The track may be doubled and the station may be in-creased to six or eight platforms, or the track may be divided up into block sections (see page 73) so that two or more trains may follow one another around the circuit. There is no particular advantage claimed for this layout, but it is a fine exercise in gradient building. The points to note are that clearance is required above the track at A-B, E-F, G-H and K-A. The point of crossing (L) may be moved about until gradients B-C, H-I and J-K are as nearly as possible equal in severity. The vertical scale of the gradient profile in fig 33 is of course many times greater than the horizontal scale in order to show up the effect.

Another possibility is to leave things as drawn and to have a high level/low level interchange station at L. Gradient H-I then restricts the length of trains for all but the most powerful locomotives; it is as well to find out about such things by drawing a gradient profile at an early stage.

Gradients may be expressed as rise over run; ie the increase in height over a length measured along the track (not the horizontal projection of it), or as a percentage. Thus a line rising at the rate of 1ft in each 100ft has a gradient of 1 in 100, or 1% or 10‰. The latter is a Continental notation.

Fig 32 Simplified plan of Peter Moore's layout: C controls; EC East Croydon station; H hidden loop lines; S Selhurst station (see fig 88).

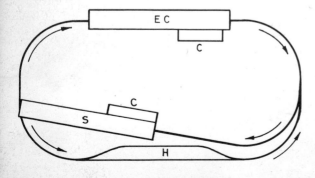

Prototype gradients are normally gentle but some fairly well-known exceptions are listed below;

Shap, BR, south of Carlisle:	1 in 75
Field Hill, CPR (Rockies):	1 in 45
Gotthard, SBB, Switzerland:	1 in 37
Raton Pass, ATSF (Rockies):	1 in 34
Folkestone Hbr, BR:	1 in 30
Sneyd Colliery, Staffs:	1 in 18
Snowdon Mountain Rly, Wales:	1 in 5.5
Pilatus Rly, Switzerland:	1 in 2

The Snowdon and Pilatus lines are rack and pinion worked and the usual limit for adhesion between metal wheels and rails is about 1 in 15, and then mainly for lightweight branch trains. Models with nylon tyres or magnetic adhesion (see fig 2) may do better than this, but with some loss of realism. Field Hill and the Gotthard both have spiral tunnels with compensation (ie a slight reduction of gradient) on sharp curves to help the locomotives.

The Mountain Subdivision (see page 7), as its name implies, has formidable gradients which reproduce operating conditions of the real CPR route through the Rockies and Selkirks. Like the prototype, it has compensation on curves; this was arrived at by reducing the rise over every 90-degree bend from 1.25in to 0.95in. The normal rise for straight track is, like that in real life, 1in for every 45in. The total rise is less than one might expect, because gradients cannot begin and end (or even change slope) abruptly; they must be rounded off smoothly. Failure to account for this at the drawing board will mean a gradient eventually constructed which is either steeper than intended or unable to gain enough height to clear another track passing underneath. As a rough guide, *at least* one coachlength should be added to the run of every steep gradient to allow for rounding off. Thus if a rise of 3in at a maximum gradient of 1 in 30 is desired, the run is increased from 3 × 30in to, say, 100in in OO scale. This allows for a coach 10in long, and 5in is added to the run at each end of the 1 in 30 gradient.

Layouts large or small may be built up using layout elements and principles described above, but there are some additional practical rules for operating convenience which should be observed. Operators should be able to see trains at all times except when in short tunnels; if not, they should be aided by indicator lights on the control panel or possibly by strategically placed mirrors. All parts of the track and preferably the baseboard too should be easily accessible for cleaning, maintenance and retrieval of derailed vehicles. Access to track in long tunnels may be through a sliding panel at the rear of the baseboard or in a backdrop; or the hills and mountains may be hollow allowing hidden access from *underneath* the baseboard. No layout plan should leave the drawing board if it requires an operator with arms six feet long to reach the most distant stretch of track.

Reference has inevitably been made to items whose design and construction will be unfamiliar to many readers; now it is time to tackle them, in greater detail.

Fig 34 Scratchbuilt roundhouse at Skunk River. The enclosed water tower was a plastic kit; next to it is Korean brass 87 (HO) 16.5 CPR T-1-c 2-10-4 No 5935.

CHAPTER FOUR

FOUNDATIONS

Model railway baseboards may be supported on kitchen tables, chests of drawers, mantelpieces or bookshelves. Ingenious schemes involve layouts which turn upside down to become beds and other useful items of furniture, or which disappear into the wall or ceiling when not required. Normally, however, one finds layouts mounted on temporary or permanent supports or sets of trestles made for the purpose. Out of doors, trestles may alternate with low stone walls (50) or with the natural terrain of a rockery.

In the garden there is often much more space available for laying out wide, sweeping curves, and lengthy trains can be admired amongst attractive scenery. In wet weather the disadvantages are obvious, although part of the layout may be accommodated in a shed or garage where at least the operator can keep dry. The line must be kept clear of leaves, mud and spreading plants; mice and hedgehogs must also be discouraged from setting up house in tunnels.

Indoors, it is equally necessary to beware of cats walking along narrow plastic bridges or jumping off the baseboard in frantic haste when a train appears. There are also problems with dampness in cellars, or with heat in summer and cold in winter in uninsulated attics and lofts. Dust is a problem, everywhere. The choice of location for the railway is therefore not so straightforward as it might at first appear, and it is very desirable indeed to ensure that all necessary repairs to walls, ceilings, floors, and household electric wiring are carried out competently before much time and money are invested in a permanent railway room.

Portable layouts may have a single baseboard with folding legs; or a folding baseboard *and* folding legs (like a superior type of paperhanger's pasting table) or a number of baseboard sections which are joined together when in use. Some baseboards or sections thereof are light enough to be carried by one person while others are designed for standing up to the rigours of exhibitions and need several people to lift them. The weight of tracks, buildings and scenery can seriously affect the portability of layouts and if tall and fragile objects such as signals or telegraph poles are positioned near the edges some

form of firm protective cover is needed during transportation. The smaller the scale adopted for the layout, the easier it is to overcome these problems; a quite extensize Z scale layout may be folded up and carried by one person while in gauge 1 there is little one could do without a pretty large baseboard.

Permanent layouts may still be built in sections with a view to taking them along when one moves house, but limitations on weight and height may be neglected. Scenery may be made from heavy but inexpensive materials, and walls may sometimes be used for background scenes. Problems with electric wiring are reduced where there is no need to interconnect sections of baseboard which may be carried and stored separately, although the better types of heavy-duty multi-pin plugs and sockets can make connecting up a relatively quick and trouble-free operation.

Closed top baseboards have a continuous flat surface, like a table. Tracks, buildings and scenery all rest on this surface, which may, however, have small areas cut out to form ponds and so on. Portable layouts are almost invariably of this type.

Open top baseboards have no continuous surface but track, scenery etc are carried on individual supports secured to timber beams and columns in the foundation frame. This is ideal for areas of undulating terrain (53) and where lines are rising and falling with little or no level track.

The L-shaped closed top baseboard (fig 35) is suitable for fitting permanently into a corner of a room. It has shelves and cupboards underneath for storing spare parts, magazines and tools. A painted background is carried on plywood or hardboard sheets and a circular hole has been let into the baseboard top to accommodate a turntable pit. The layout is of the end-to-end type and two operators could sit at separate control panels mounted at each end of the structure.

Rectangular closed top baseboard fig 36 goes in the centre of a room because it is too wide for an operator to reach across it from one side and all-round access is needed. It is of simple but robust construction, with a track configuration

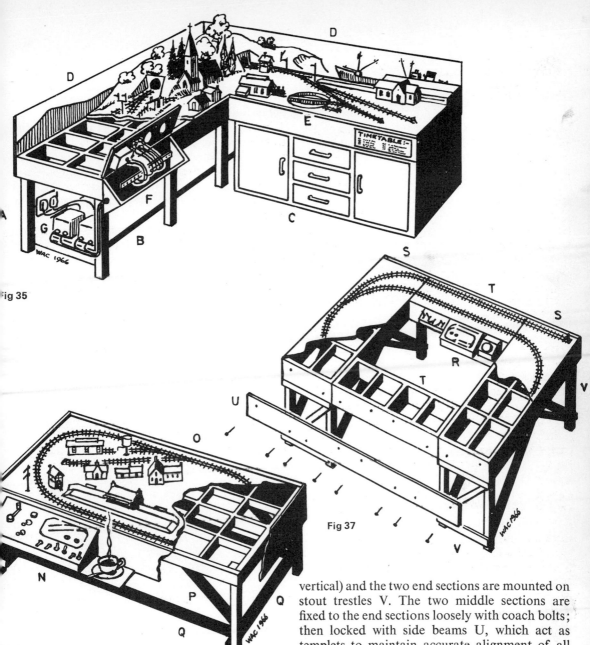

Fig 35

Fig 37

Fig 36

permitting continuous running. Thick plywood, strip O, supports the controller and control panel N; it is also raised up to prevent derailed vehicles running over the edge and dropping 250 scale feet to the floor.

Sectional closed top baseboard fig 37 would suit an exhibition type gauge O or 1 layout. It is built from wide timbers laid on edge to give maximum resistance to bending in any vertical plane (in engineering terms, their major axes are

vertical) and the two end sections are mounted on stout trestles V. The two middle sections are fixed to the end sections loosely with coach bolts; then locked with side beams U, which act as templets to maintain accurate alignment of all sections one to another; and finally secured by tightening up the loose bolts. It may take time to carry out these operations, but such a structure will give trouble-free service at exhibitions and will stand a lot of knocking about. Operators inside at control panel R can reach all parts of the layout, while visitors can walk all round the outside, watching the trains and asking questions.

Square closed top baseboard fig 38 is shown (with typical dimensions) as a free-standing permanent structure; by removing braces E, F

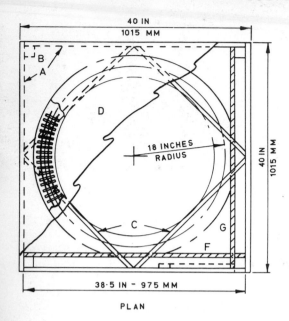

PLAN

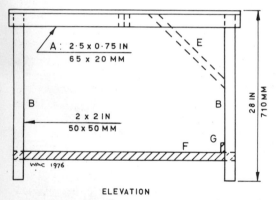

ELEVATION

Fig 38 SIMPLE CLOSED BASEBOARD

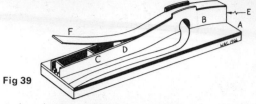

Fig 39

A raised trackbed is carried on an embankment or stone causeway in fig 39. The plan of trackbed B is drawn on baseboard section A and spacers C and D are glued in place. They should taper inwards slightly towards the top to avoid any danger of the finished walls leaning outwards. That would never do. Side walls E are both cut out at the same time, matched carefully to see they are the same shape (with allowance for differences in circumference between inside and outside arcs on a sharp curve) and glued in place. Pins or clamps may be needed to hold them in position while the glue sets; after this the trackbed F is cut to shape and fitted. A piece of brown paper held firmly over the tops of the side walls and creased along the edges makes a good paper pattern or templet, and the trackbed is made slightly oversize so that it can be trimmed to an exact fit after the glue has set. Leave at least twelve hours before trimming; it is better to be safe than sorry.

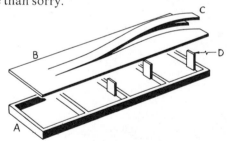

Fig 40

and G (which it may not need if the carpentry is good and if it is well treated) and replacing the fixed legs B with folding ones it is easily turned into a portable baseboard. Anything larger than this is difficult for one person to carry.

Braces, when fitted, are fixed to both sides of each leg; the drawing merely shows one of each type as examples. In the upper drawing the top cover D is a single sheet of plywood or composition material, on to which the trackbed of cork or other simulated ballast is laid. Note how the diagonals C meet at the centre points of side frames A, so that the circle of track is directly supported by main timbers and not by a flat sheet which could act as a sounding board, amplifying train noises with unpleasant booming or drumming sounds.

The start of a gradient is shown in fig 40, where a curved section C is partly cut out from a baseboard section B. The baseboard must be reasonably flexible, for example $\frac{3}{8}$in ply; chipboard would not flex at all. Here the trackbed rests directly on spacers such as D, which is the first to be fixed in position if the desired height is known (as it will be if the adjoining section of baseboard and trackbed are already made). An intermediate spacer is then fitted with the top sheet B and C held in position temporarily, and adjusted until the desired gradient is obtained at the higher end of the slope. Both spacers are now finally fixed in place and the top sheet is glued or nailed down on to frame A. The remaining spacers are now fixed, the lower end of the slope

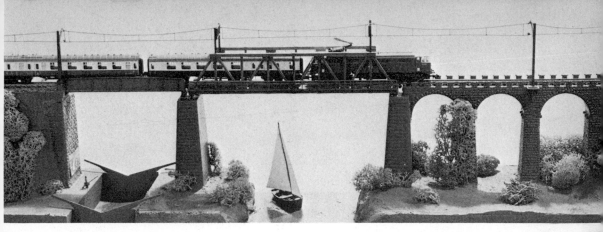

Fig 41 Baseboards have depressed sections for waterways, like the Grand Reunion Canal *(left)* and the Great Ooze. All the N scale bridges shown were plastic kits.

curving off gently with the natural bend of the material. The number of spacers shown is suitable for a soft or thin top sheet; with firmer material fewer spacers are required.

Fig 42

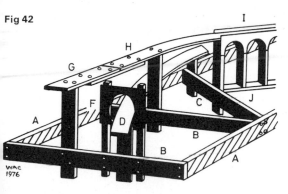

Open top baseboard fig 42 has main side frames A with perpendicular cross braces B and angled one C. Careful cutting of timber is needed here to ensure tight joints so that the raised trackbed G, H and I will be firmly supported; it must not sway about when trains pass over. Sections G and H are spliced together with a short strip of trackbed material, and I rests on a viaduct whose columns are carried firmly by secondary brace J.

Not only the trackbed has to be supported off the main frame or bracing timbers; so do objects like tunnel mouth F over trackbed D. Scenery contours are produced with chicken wire and/or other means, with a freedom to use space above *and below* track level which is not possible with a closed top baseboard. (See Chapter Seven).

L-girder type baseboard construction, fig 43, has advantages in some circumstances as trimmers D and E can not only act as braces for the main girders A/B but can extend to support edg-

ing strip G of any shape required. Main timbers A are mounted to legs C with their major, or YY, axes vertical (as shown at H) to resist downward forces and weights; to reinforce them against sideways forces strips B are glued and screwed on to them to form an inverted L shape. This forms a beam having strength in both XX and YY directions and capable of spanning longer distances without intermediate support than the main frames in fig 42 assuming similar sizes of timbers are used. If the space beneath the frames is to be divided up by cupboards the L girder loses some of its advantages, but trimmers such as D can be fixed to the strip B with just one screw at each side.

Trackbed F needs close supports because it is curved; if straight it could run a long way on its own miniature L girder.

L-girder structure dimensions are given in fig 44 for a typical arrangement of L girders A attached to legs B, with diagonal braces C and crossbraces D between the legs. Such a structure can be 20ft or more long if desired; the sizes of

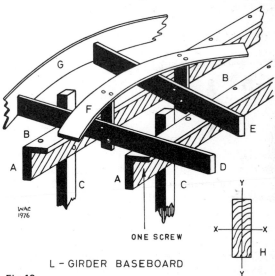

ONE SCREW

L – GIRDER BASEBOARD

Fig 43

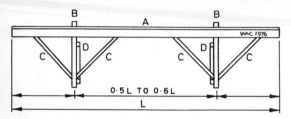

Fig 44 L - GIRDER STRUCTURE DIMENSIONS

timbers used are best left to discussion with a timber merchant, although for general guidance the larger component of a long L girder should not be less than 3 × 1 in (75 × 25mm) and sizes of legs and cross braces should not be less than those shown in fig 38.

Baseboard materials should preferably be light, strong, non-warping and easy to cut and to stick pins and screws into. Not all materials have all these properties, but Sundeala, Weyroc and other specially made composition boards come close to the ideal. Plywood and hardboard do not take pins and screws easily, and small pilot holes have to be drilled before a screw will bite.

Warping is unlikely with good quality plywood but is very likely with hardboard as the temperature and humidity of the atmosphere change. Hardboard can be used quite successfully, however, if it is 'killed' by storing in a slightly damp atmosphere or if it is thoroughly moistened with a wet rag on the rough side about half an hour before being fixed to the timber frame. When it dries it tries to shrink, but the screws or panel pins which are driven home every few inches all round the edge hold it back and as a result it pulls itself taut and much of its tendency to warp is removed. It can still act as a resonating board for train noises, but if the timber supports are fixed directly underneath the tracks and the tracks are mounted loosely on sound-absorbing underlay material the results are every bit as satisfactory as on other materials. Both hardboard and thin plywood need well bracing.

Really soft composition materials, such as wood fibre insulation board, tend to be flammable and to fray badly at the edges. The answer is to keep them away from fires and electrical equipment which might overheat or spark (sheets of bakelite, mica or paxolin should be used as shields where required) and to fit a thin strip of hardwood or plywood all round the edge of the baseboard; this not only makes a neat finishing touch but also acts as a safety barrier.

Timber for the framework should be straight, close-grained, free from cracks, knots, pieces of bark, rough saw-marks and cross-graining, and should be reasonably well seasoned. Anti-rot and anti-woodworm fluids may be brushed on, especially at holes and joints, if timber in the vicinity shows susceptibility to attack. Woodworms are especially fond of rough or loose joints and centrally-heated lofts where ventilation is poor.

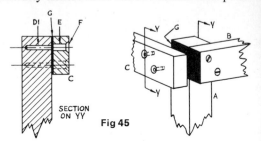

Fig 45

Methods of joining timber which require no knowledge of real carpentry are screwing and glueing fig 45. A post A is to be fixed in the angle formed by two beams B and C, and the mating surfaces are first sandpapered smooth and flat. In the sketch it is beam C which is about to be fixed in place, and the section on YY shows what you would see if beam C were to be cut through the upper screw-hole. Note that the lower screw-hole is shown in dotted line because it is some distance behind the plane of the section (or cut). This is a basic principle of technical drawing. The section shows something which is not clear from the general sketch; the holes D1 and D2 are drilled slightly smaller than the outside diameter of the screw and almost the whole of the way through the post. The hole E in the beam C is then opened out to the same size as the outside diameter of the screw and countersunk (F) just sufficiently to allow the head of the screw to bed itself in comfortably, flush with the surface of the timber or slightly below this. This makes a neat, strong joint without splitting the wood. You can obtain special drills which do all this in one drilling operation for some of the popular sizes.

To ensure that the holes are drilled correctly in both pieces of wood, it is advisable to hold them with a carpenter's cramp while the first hole is being drilled. The screw can then be inserted and the cramp moved so that the other hole can be drilled. It is not necessary to screw up the cramp with great force, crushing the wood; just nip it up until the mating surfaces are firmly held together, prop the other end of the horizontal beam on a chair or table, rest the post against some firm object and start drilling. Watch out when you drill the holes for C that they do not meet the screws at right angles through B.

To make the joint extra strong, remove screws, sandpaper off any rough edges or burrs caused by drilling, and apply a thin, even coat of any modern cold-spreading glue to both mating surfaces. Replace screws, nipping them up tight without too much brute force and without twisting the tip of the screwdriver.

When two light pieces of wood have to be joined and it is not possible to obtain the required strength by ordinary means, metal straps and brackets can be used. These are in addition to screws and glue and are added after the joint is made.

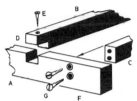

Fig 46

Joints for cross-braces (fig 46) should be made by halving, but a simple screwed joint F will suffice if excessive weight is not rested on the crossbeam. The halved joint D is made by cutting a step out of the end of beam B and exactly the same sized step out of beam A. If B does not make a perfectly accurate and tight fit in A the joint will be a source of weakness and the glue will not bond itself properly to all the mating surfaces. The screw E is fitted to hold the joint while the glue sets.

The crossbeam C must be cut to exactly the right length so that it fits the space between the two main beams which it spans. If it is made too long or too short it will cause the main frame to buckle, and a weak joint is likely if its ends are not quite square and flat. Screws G are inserted through holes drilled and countersunk as in fig 45F; note that screws grip less firmly in the end of a piece of wood than they do when inserted into the side (across the grain) so use longer screws, or a smaller pilot drill, or only drill into the wood half as far as shown in fig 45D. Some extra strength can also be obtained if one or both of the holes is drilled at a slight angle, cutting across the grain instead of running parallel with it.

A wall-mounted baseboard, fig 47D, on frame C, rests its weight mainly on pieces of wood screwed to the wall and not, as in other cases, entirely on the floor. Posts A are first fixed to the

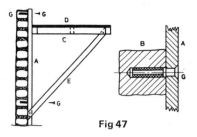

Fig 47

wall and the frame is then screwed to these, with diagonal supports E to prevent twisting.

To fix posts A to the wall a hole G is first drilled in solid stone, concrete block or brick B (plaster is too soft and will not grip properly) using a special masonry drill bit of the correct size for the Rawlplug or other proprietary plugging material. The plug does not completely fill the hole in the wall. The post A is clearance drilled and countersunk. Two plugged holes per post should suffice on most walls, but more can be added at will; if the wall is not straight it may be necessary to fit a small piece of packing timber between the post and the wall to maintain correct alignment. If this is done be sure to drill clearance holes in the packer to avoid splitting it. Posts and diagonals are needed at about 3ft intervals for conventional closed top baseboards; much longer spans are possible with L-girder construction.

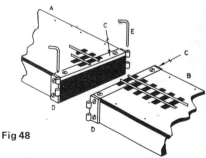

Fig 48

Portable baseboard section joints are used when sections of a portable baseboard have to be joined or separated many times, in the shortest possible time. In fig 48 there are two sections A and B ready for joining. Half hinges D are fitted where necessary and convenient and a special pin E is inserted in each hinge when the two halves come together. Pin E is made from a piece of steel or brass rod which just pushes smoothly into place without force or slackness (that is, a push fit). The tip is rounded off so that it is easy to insert. The hinges have to withstand quite a bit of knocking about and twisting in the course of transportation, assembly and dismantling at exhibitions and so on, and a heavy machine-made hinge is desirable. Good quality brass hinges are used on yachts and ships, and a boat chandler's store is a good place to look for them. A strip of hard material C is fitted, to which the track ends are lightly but firmly secured.

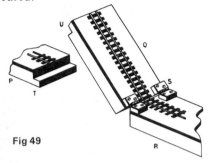

Fig 49

Lifting sections of baseboard present problems of lining up two track joints, and fig 49 shows one way to do it. Lifting section Q is hinged at one end to R and rests on P when lowered. Hinges S are raised to allow the rail ends to be a close fit without risking interference between them during opening and closing of the joint. If the hinges were below rail level, the rails

Fig 50 The down Red Dragonfly speeds past a slow goods train on a pond-side wall. Plastic-bodied 76(OO)16.5 models like these are excellent for beginners.

would hit each other on lifting. The end U is sloped sufficiently to avoid interference as it comes to rest on step T, also making a tight fit. It is an easy matter to run flexible electric wiring under Q to take power (through a pair of holes in the board) to the rails. When a section of baseboard or track, or a bridge, is removed it is often necessary to arrange spring brass contacts at either end to pass on the electric supplies, and to fit press studs, half hinges or some other form of limit stops to align both ends of the movable track accurately.

Outdoor foundations, photograph 50, need above all to be firm and dry. The simplest type carries a track on timber planks screwed to posts driven into the ground. The whole timber structure should be treated with creosote or some other preparation to protect it against rot and bad weather, after which it may be partially buried by rocks, earth and small plants until it appears to be part of the surrounding terrain. Low walls may be edges of an ornamental flower-bed or pool where derailments must be avoided by careful installation. Good drainage must prevent mud and water washing over the track, so bricks or small stone blocks are laid on a firm base of crushed stone, with more of the same at the side. In addition, small gaps may be left between the bricks to allow rain water to run away during extra-heavy downpours.

CHAPTER FIVE

TRACKWORK AND POWER SUPPLY

Trackwork means the track on which trains run, together with all the associated equipment for changing directions of travel. It supports the weight of locomotives and trains, guides their wheels into predetermined paths and in model form usually serves as a means of conducting electricity which is picked up through locomotive and railcar wheels. In full size practice too, one part of the electric traction circuit of electric trains usually passes through the wheels to the rails, although not quite in the same way.

Mechanically, the functions of trackwork are to provide a stable path for train wheels which is always of the correct gauge and which does not change direction suddenly. These may seem obvious attributes, but failure to check them carefully is responsible for many derailments.

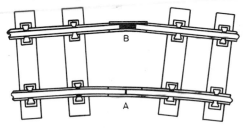

Fig 51   LOOSE RAIL JOINTS

Loose rail joints fig 51B are prevalent on badly-laid curves and provide wheels with an easy escape route. Buckled and twisted rails may make the gauge too narrow, causing the wheels to bind; and they interfere with electrical pick-up when some wheels are unable to remain in contact with the rails. A low spot (fig 52A), a high spot (fig 52B) and a twist (fig 52C) all contribute to bad running and it may not be long before fibre or plastic lug D on the sleeper is unable to grip the rail at all.

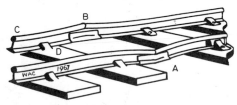

Fig 52   BUCKLED RAILS

To promote reliable operation, track should always be checked before and after laying with a track gauge to see that the rails are correctly spaced, and with a yard- or metre-length straight edge to see there are no kinks or subtle changes of gradient. Level track should also be checked with a spirit level, and track on a steady gradient should be checked with a spirit level resting on a templet whose upper surface is level and whose lower surface is inclined at the correct angle of the gradient. Strict track discipline is essential if fast and heavy traffic is to be displayed with confidence to admiring visitors.

Diesel and electric locomotives with bogie-mounted driving mechanisms can easily adapt themselves to uneven track, and so can well designed steam locomotives with spring suspension on all driving and carrying wheels. In spite of its great length, the Selkirk 2-10-4 shown in photograph 75 will glide serenely round curves and over crossings where a simple 0-6-0T quickly comes to grief. There are, however, many more 0-6-0Ts in service on model railway layouts than Selkirks, and moreover springing is not used for inexpensive model locomotives so it is for the smaller engine with no springs that model trackwork is usually designed.

In Chapter Two it was said that we must not use too strict a definition of a scale model because of practical difficulties; the difficulties envisaged are those involved in laying and maintaining trackwork to the degree of accuracy required for the operation of trains having scale size wheels. Indeed if you are going to have everything exactly to scale, with wheel treads and flanges to scale, then your standards of track laying must be unusually high. In full size practice a variation of $\frac{1}{2}$in in track gauge or in cross level is a major fault. Just scale *that* down to OO or HO, or even N, and you will see the standard of accuracy that will be needed. Such wheels are themselves unacceptably fragile for most modellers and it is thus customary to make wheels *and* track very much more robust than exact scale size. There are NEM (European) and NMRA (American) standard sheets detailing the design of almost every technical aspect of railway modelling but it is

Fig 53 Cache Lake junction, CPR, with *(left to right)* a Royal Hudson 4-6-4; a GP7 'hood' diesel; and a D-10-g 4-6-0 with four F7 GM-EMD 'cab' diesels heading up 51 freight cars on Peco Streamline track.

not necessary to study them in detail. All one needs to know is that models made to NEM or NMRA standards should be compatible in respect of their wheels, rail profiles and electrical connections. NMRA wheel and rail profiles are finer than NEM, so although NMRA models will run reasonably well on NEM track the converse is not always true. As for models whose wheels and rails do not exactly conform to either standards, one must take care not to purchase large quantities of unknown makes without first trying out a few samples.

As a rough guide, the degree of closeness to scale dimensions adopted for various standards and by well-known manufacturers follows this order:

1 Exact scale
2 Protofour; Shinohara Code 70
3 British fine scale
4 NMRA RP 12
5 Peco Streamline; Code 100
6 NEM Rivarossi, Märklin, Fleischmann (new production)
7 Triang-Hornby; Wrenn, Lima, Jouef, Trix

It must be emphasised that this is only a rough

Fig 54 Track and Wheels:

For satisfactory running, dimension A must be less than the track gauge but B must be correct or the wheel flanges will foul check rails at turnouts etc. So B must be greater than C. Rail height D must be sufficient to allow wheel flanges to clear all obstructions; excessive height impairs realism and causes rough running over turnouts and crossings E, F and J affect realism only. K is a British type cast chair supporting bullhead rail; L is a tie-plate supporting Vignoles (flat-bottom) rail. The sleeper, or crosstie, is wood. At M however the rails are soldered to 'printed-circuit' copper-clad insulated material with small amounts of solder on the *outsides* of the rails. The copper surface is broken at N to prevent short circuits between the rails (on two-rail systems; see fig 133). O is a rail joiner, or fishplate.

G is an axle-box with parallel bearing; H has needle-point bearing which, though more delicate, is more free-running. Insulation I for two-rail systems is of two types; a central hub bush *(left)* or a ring inserted between wheel centre and outer tyre *(right)*. The ring type is best for locomotives as all parts attached to the wheel centre are isolated from the rails and cannot cause short circuits if properly adjusted.

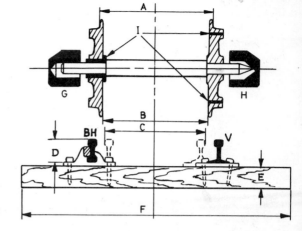

Fundamental Track Measurements:

1 Rail weight (lbs/yard):

BR	109 & 98
Talyllyn	40 & 45
Mersey Docks	126 & 75
FS	121 & 54
CNR & CPR	130 & 85
NYC	159, 127, 105, 90 & 80

2 Due to variations in (1) above, rail height D varies. Prototype FS 'type 50' rail is 148mm high; this is 1.7mm in 1 : 87 (HO) scale but NEM123 specifies 2.5mm for HO; 3.5mm for gauge O; and 5mm for gauge 1. British and North American model rail is usually described as 'code 100' for 0.1-in or 2.54mm; 'code 70' for 0.07-in or 1.78mm (for greater realism in HO or OO scales); 'code 55' for 0.055-in or 1.4mm (for smaller scales) and 'code 125' or 0.125-in for larger scales.

3 Spacing of sleepers, or crossties J varies too:

BR	5.5 × 9.5-in cross section by 8.5ft long at 30in centres.
FS	23.5 to 29.5in centres.
CPR	20 to 22in centres.
USA	15 to 18in centres on industrial shortlines.
n-g	36in centres on Talyllyn narrow-gauge line.

guide and not a strict analysis; makers introduce new and improved products all the time and standards generally have improved enormously since World War II.

NMRA standards have the most widespread acceptance, being used almost exclusively throughout North America and by most Japanese, Korean and European suppliers to the North American market. There are, however, American-outline models on sale with NEM wheels; some North American modellers dislike them but many European modellers operate North American models on their layouts, and they prefer them with NEM wheels.

The tables and diagrams in fig 54 show the more important dimensions of rails and track, and for a proper understanding some comments are necessary. Prototype rail used this century

has been of the Vignoles or flat-bottomed type (fig 54V) everywhere except in Britain up to about 1960. British lines used the bullhead type (fig 54BH) with cast iron chairs and wooden or metal keys (fig 54K) to support the rail and hold it in place. There was no sudden cut-off point, bullhead rail still being used on some principal lines, branch lines and in sidings. Rail height, width and weight per unit length vary considerably from very light narrow-gauge or branch lines to heavy-duty main lines in Canada and the USA.

Crossties or sleepers are usually of wood, but concrete or a mixture of concrete and steel are gradually becoming the normal type on high speed routes. The spacing of crossties varies from railway to railway, but some typical examples are given in fig 54. The ballast used may also vary greatly, from a thick bed of crushed rock on fast lines to a thin layer of ashes in yards and sidings.

Model rails are made of solid drawn brass or nickel silver, or of plated steel. Cheaper varieties may use thin sheet brass or tinplate (tinned steel plate) bent to shape. Of these, solid drawn nickel silver best resists corrosion and accidental damage; brass is easiest to solder but tarnishes fairly rapidly unless in constant use; plated steel is vulnerable to corrosion once cut or damaged but enables locomotives fitted with magnetic aids to gain extra adhesion.

Model crossties are made of wood, fibre or plastic and the latter often have integrally moulded chairs or spikes which hold the rail in position (and maintain the correct track gauge). Fibre crossties do not hold the rails very firmly and they are usually reinforced with short metal staples which grip the rail. Wooden ones sometimes used for the larger gauges of O and 1 must have separate cast metal chairs or drawn metal spikes and tieplates (fig 54L). Rails can also be soldered to the heads of brass pins or nails driven into the trackbed, or to copper clad insulating material serving as sleepers.

Model track ballast is made from rock chippings, granulated cork or foam plastic underlay. The latter is formed to the right shape, complete with regular depressions into which the crossties fit. Each maker has a special underlay for each type of track and one must take care to obtain the right one. Little air bubbles trapped in the spongy plastic material act as springs and damp out vibration and noise; but not when clogged up with paint or glue, or pressed flat beneath track held down with screws. Rock chippings etc are a nuisance when they get into moving parts of trackwork or locomotives and they do not act as dampers to the same degree (if at all). A cork or balsa wood underlay is satisfactory where foam plastic strip cannot be used (under-moving parts of turnouts, for instance) and has some sound-reducing effect.

Sectional or 'snap' track comes assembled in lengths which are to the maker's own standard, either curved or straight, and it usually has rail joiners (fishplates) fitted ready for instant connection to another section of track. This is the type of track that comes in train sets, but can also be bought separately. Using this type of track in conjunction with the maker's book of track plans it is possible to set up a layout in no time. The snag is that one is compelled to use curves of the radius provided, so that odd radius curves and transition curves are ruled out. Some types of sectional track have integral crossties and ballast or trackbed formed in wood, plastic or tinplate.

Flexible track is made in yard or metre lengths, with plastic crossties inter-connected on alternate sides, so that resistance to curving the track is small. It enables one to obtain any form of simple or compound curve, but the rails are the same length only when the track is straight and one of them has to be cut when it is curved. Some prototype railways use parallel rail joints and others stagger them; prototype rail lengths vary from about 33ft to 66ft, or 200ft for short lengths of welded rail. Most modellers are content to adopt parallel rail joints just where they occur rather than reproduce scale lengths, and leave it to turnouts and crossings to produce the characteristic clatter of wheels.

Installation of flexible track involves lining it up to the preceding section of track, cutting it to length if necessary and securing it to the trackbed or baseboard. The desired curve is obtained in the track and the piece of rail to be cut off is marked with a slight saw cut *before* any plastic crossties are removed. The track is disconnected and removed to a workbench for sawing with a fine-toothed or razor saw, making sure that the rails are not bent badly in the process. Now the first two crossties back from the sawcut are removed, leaving a short section of rail protruding on both sides when the track is curved. All ends (whether recently sawn or not) must be trimmed with a smooth file and all burrs or sharp edges must be lightly rounded off.

A section of underlay is now fitted to the underside of the track, lightly glued underneath each rail only, not smothered with glue. The track is joined to the preceding section (which may have to be lifted a bit to let the underlay find its right place) and curved to final position. The outside edges of the underlay are lifted and lightly glued before being pressed gently down to the trackbed or baseboard. Small but heavy objects (such as locomotives) are parked all along the newly laid track and left there overnight, and that is another job done. The gaps left by removing the last two crossties may be filled with pieces of wood or by copper-clad bakelite ties which are lightly soldered to the rails to preserve the exact track gauge. Alternatively, instead of removing crossties it is possible

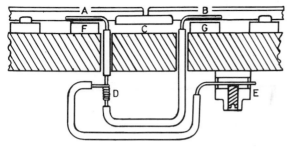

Fig 55 Rails A and B are mechanically connected by rail joiner C. A U-shaped bonding wire is soldered to both rails, allowing rails to expand *freely*. A feeder wire may be wrapped around and soldered at D; it is run *loosely* to terminal block E. Sleepers, or ties, F and G are positioned after soldering operations if likely to be distorted by heat.

Transition curves connect tangent (straight) track to circular track, as previously described in Chapter Three. The formulae and construction are given in *Model Railway News* for October 1964, but a length of flexible track will take up a reasonably smooth transitional shape if one end is soldered to the tangent track and the other end is curved.

Superelevation (or cant) is the height by which the outside rail on a curve is raised relative to the inside rail to counteract the overturning effect. This may be as much as six inches on British main lines. It is zero where the transition curve begins and increases steadily to the maximum amount where it merges into a circular curve.

to saw away the top portion of them to allow clearance for the rail joiners.

Power to locomotives is fed from the control panel or control unit through electric cables to some point where they are mechanically secured to the rails; thereafter the rails act as conductors and any high-resistance path such as a loose rail joiner causes a loss of voltage and consequently a drop in speed as trains pass that point. To avoid this, rail joints may be soldered or bridged with short bonding wires soldered to the rails (55). On straight track it is best to use bonding wires, leaving small gaps between ends of rails to allow for thermal expansion during a very hot summer. If this is overlooked, rails will buckle and distort. On curves, there is usually sufficient give in the foam plastic underlay to permit sideways movement, and it is safe to solder up joints (51A) to prevent rails springing out of the true curved path as in fig 51B. If the track fails to settle down correctly after all joints are soldered it is often wise to hold a hot soldering iron against the most highly-stressed joiner to allow it to creep slightly.

Curvature is checked with plywood or hardboard templets cut to the correct curvature of the inside rail; they are marked out by using long trammels or a piece of string whose length equals the desired radius of curvature, allowing for a loop at one end to hold a pencil.

Straightness of straight track is checked with a yard or metre straight edge, or by eye. Squinting along the track from one end to the other with light shining on the surfaces of the rails shows up any dips, kinks or wiggles. A very long run of track may also be checked by stretching a piano wire along it, under a suitable tension.

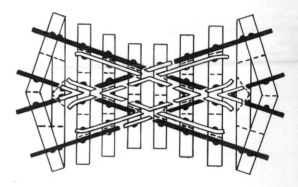

Fig 56 Black rails are live, white ones are dead to prevent short circuits from positive to negative supplies in a two-rail system. Dotted lines indicate saw- or file-cuts in a copper surface to isolate live rails from *all* other rails which might be in contact with metal wheels.

Crossings are made from straight or curved running (stock) rail and have check rails provided to guide the wheels of passing trains where they pass over gaps in the rail (fig 56). The rails are cut to prevent short circuits from one rail to another, either directly or through the wheels of trains.

Turnouts enable the paths of trains to be switched from one direction to another. The moving parts are the switch blades (fig 57B) and the place where the two inner fixed rails diverge is called the frog (fig 57D) in model practice, but a common crossing in full size terminology. British modellers use the name points for all turnouts, while North Americans call them switches; the technical name is used here to avoid confusion. Turnouts are facing when trains approach them in the direction switch-to-frog, and trailing if in the reverse direction.

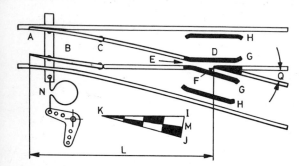

Sidings are approached by trailing turnouts wherever possible, as a fast express might be accidentally routed on to a siding by incorrect operation of a facing turnout. Turnouts are classified as left-hand if the secondary line curves away from the main (straight or less curved) line to the left in the facing direction; right-hand if to the right and a Y turnout if both lines diverge at similar curvatures. Turnouts in which there are *two* diverging lines from a main line are described as three-way.

Fig 57 Turnout parts; A is the toe of switch B. C is the heel. D is the frog or crossing, shown black to indicate those parts which are insulated in dead-frog turnouts. E is the throat; F the point of the frog. G are wing rails. Check rails H help to steady wheel pairs passing over the gap between throat and point. The extent of divergence from straight or tangent track is expressed by the frog angle Q, by the radius of curvature of the diverging track, or by the frog number. A No 4 frog, for instance, has one unit of divergence IJ in four units of length KM, measured at the frog. To specify exactly, the length of lead L is also needed. 'Omega wire' N connected to the operating bar allows the bell crank a small amount of overtravel, thus ensuring firm contact at the switch toes in both positions of the turnout.

Fig 58 Trackwork types; *(front row, left to right)*; Fleischmann 87(N)9 track with integral moulded 'ballast' and electrical uncoupling ramp. Peco 9mm (narrow)-gauge dead-frog l h turnout. Peco Streamline 16.5mm gauge med-radius (approx No 6) live- or dead-frog rh turnout. A 5p coin on Fleischmann 87(HOn) 16.5 dead-frog lh curved turnout with integral operating solenoid. A 102(TT)12 fibre-base live-frog turnout. *(Back row, left to right)*; Gintzel 87(HO)16.5 kit-built live-frog fibre-base double slip (Perspex parts do not show against balsa underlay). 16.5mm fibre-base track altered so that narrow-g trains can run on third rail. FS Venice ticket on Gintzel turnout kit parts. Eggerbahn 9mm light contractor's narrow-g track. Shinohara 87(HO)10.5 No 4 l h turnout.

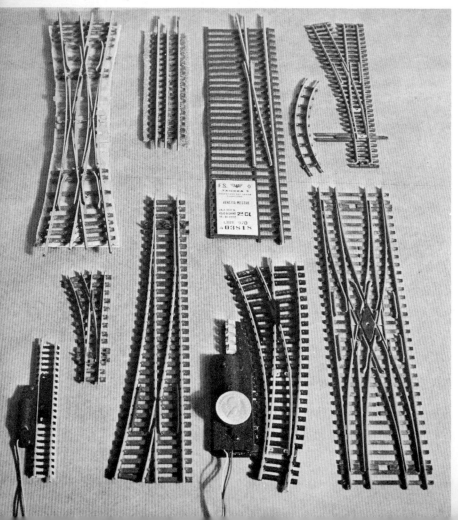

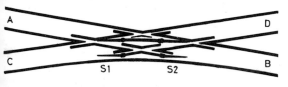

Fig 59 Single slip.

Single slips are crossings of small frog angle, having curved lines interconnecting one side of the intersecting lines via two sets of switch blades (fig 59). They permit trains to run on three different routes.

Double slips are similar but have curved rails and additional switch blades on both sides of the intersection; they permit trains to run on four different routes. They are equivalent to a pair of turnouts placed with the switch blades facing one another but occupy less space.

Catch points, traps, or derails (fig 21) are used where runaway vehicles might cause danger to other traffic. They may be set to allow trains to pass through safely, or to derail runaways. Catch points on double track lines are usually placed in the line on, or at the foot of, a gradient so that trains meet them in the trailing direction and push them closed; a light spring holds them open at all other times. They are set to derail runaway wagons running backwards. Spring catch points cannot be used on single lines where trains run both ways and they need to be operated like turnouts. Trap points too are always worked. They are placed at exits from sidings and loops to divert runaway vehicles which might otherwise foul the main line.

Turntables and traversers are varieties of movable bridges, described in Chapter Six.

Rack and pinion or cogwheel lines for steep mountain ascents have a central rack between the rails, on which engages special gear wheels fitted to locomotive axles; these make it difficult to use normal type turnouts and the problem is solved by using stub switches in which the whole section of track is pivoted (fig 60) or moved bodily sideways, as in a traverser switch (fig 61).

Fleischmann market a rack and pinion set using plastic rack moulded integral with the crossties, and any short length of track may easily be converted into a stub switch or sector table.

Check rails, which guide the inside edges of wheel flanges on sharp curves, are fitted as close to running rails as possible without causing wheels to bind. On many high bridges or viaducts, however, check rails are fitted which have much greater clearances from running rails (19, 53). Their purpose is to prevent derailed wheels or bogies ('trucks' in North America) from running off the line altogether.

Buffer stops or bumpers are fitted at the ends of sidings to prevent trains or vehicles over-running them. At important terminus stations they may be massive structures with hydraulic damping, capable of stopping from low speed a heavy train whose brakes have failed; in sidings they may be just a timber crib filled with stones or a simple frame made by bending old rails. Sand drags are sometimes used to slow down and stop runaways diverted off the line by catch points, or by trap points at siding outlets, or sometimes ahead of buffer stops at terminal stations. Real loose sand or powder should not be used on a model as it will ruin motors, gears and other mechanisms if it gets inside.

Third and fourth rails are used where trains of several different gauges use the same track fig 60 or where electrical current is collected without using running rails or overhead catenary wires. Complications arise at turnouts and crossings, in the former case, but the use of stub switches simplifies matters (although frogs or crossings are necessarily of complex designs). Where third and fourth rails are used for electrical supply, they are interrupted for part of the

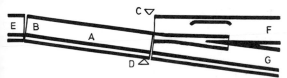

Fig 60 Mixed-gauge stub switch A pivots at B. It is shown set for travel from E to G, held against stop D. When held against C it allows travel E to F. Without track E it is a 'sector table'.

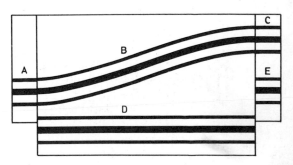

Fig 61 Rack line traverser allows travel via ABC or, when traversed, ADE.

length of the turnout or crossing, and all loco-motives and railcars require at least two pick-up points spaced far enough apart to bridge the gaps (see 135 and 136).

Current collection by model trains is usually achieved through the wheels and running rails, in the two-rail system; but stud contact is also employed, especially by Märklin and certain other Continental makers. In this system, which has largely replaced conventional third-rail, a slider fitted underneath the locomotive is pressed down by a light spring on to the heads of studs fitted between the running rails (and at a lower level; except at turnouts and crossings, where the studs rise up high enough to lift the slider clear of all rails where it might cause short circuits).

In the two-rail system, all wheels on one side of the locomotive are insulated from their axles, and thus from the chassis (see Chapter Ten) while in the third-rail system this is unnecessary. There is, however, the Trix Express arrangement using a third rail and locomotives insulated on *both* sides; this enables two locomotives to be separately controlled (by two controllers) on the same track at one time. Electric prototype loco-motives collecting current from overhead wires through trolleys or pantographs can be operated on third-rail track; or on two-rail (if insulated on one side to prevent shorting across two-rail power supplies) or on Trix Express tracks as a *third* independent motive power unit on a single track (if insulated on both sides).

Methods of wheel insulation are shown in fig 54 and methods of current collection in fig 133. Stud contact track appears in 11 (Märklin lay-out), 4 (Bridgewater) and 31 (Knoll's Green).

Turnouts may be operated by simple mechani-cal means as shown for a signal in fig 121, but remote electrical control is more satisfactory when interlocking is required. In fig 150, an engine going the whole length of sections 2 and 3 must traverse three turnouts, all three of which may be correctly set by pressing one button. By interconnecting solenoids and relays, pressing one button can establish a path through large numbers of turnouts in a busy marshalling yard or pas-senger station. At Skunk River or Whiskeyjack one traces any desired train path along the lines on the mimic diagram, pressing all buttons in that path; this sets all turnouts correctly. Another variation is to mount terminals in the track lines on a mimic diagram, so that when touched with an electric pencil connected to one

side of the ac supply they feed one side of the turnout solenoid concerned. This is a simple and effective way of operating turnouts.

Solenoids may be continuously rated (in which case the power to them may be left on) or momentarily rated. Most model railway solen-oids are of the latter type and require 'passing contact' switches which cannot stay permanently closed. A superior arrangement is to charge a large capacitor through a current-limiting resistor and then to discharge it through the solenoid. The capacitor charges up to the peak ac voltage 149K), which is higher than the nominal 15–20V rms value. Once discharged, the capacitor takes time to recharge, and if the switch is left closed in the circuit to the solenoid the current which flows is insufficient to burn out the coils, because of the resistor in the circuit. Complete units are available commercially (photo 129).

Electrical sectioning of trackwork is shown in fig 64, where common problems are met and solutions given. Electrical features of turnouts with dead or live frogs are shown in 57 and 63 respectively; and of a crossing in 62.

Common return wiring is shown in 64; where its limitations on return loops are evident; a reliable method of wiring return loops is shown. (See also fig 150 for further information on track sectioning.)

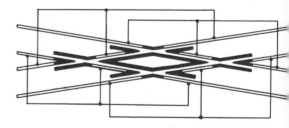

Fig 62 Dead-frog crossing sections (black) are insulated from live rails (white) so electrical connections (light lines) can be permanent. Live frogs need switches as in 63C.

Fig 63 Live turnout frog A cannot be fed permanently from either rail without short circuits in one position or another. Feeding via blades as at B causes sparking and worse if dirt intervenes, but auxiliary switch C attached to the operating bar (or solenoid; see fig 122) is more reliable and can replace track section switches on the control panel in some circum-stances. Rail joiners I *must* be insulated, but N may be metal.

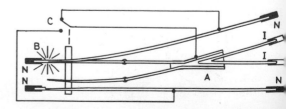

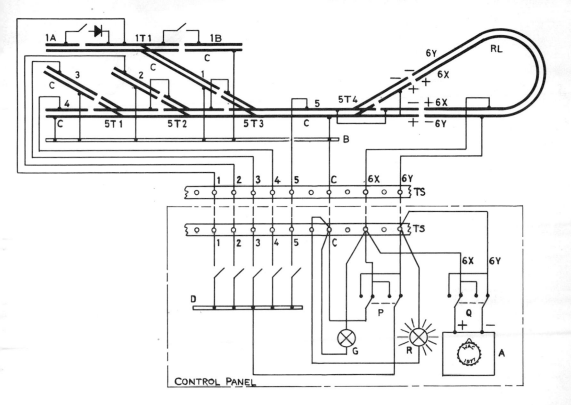

CONTROL PANEL

Fig 64 Turnout problems (live- or dead-frog) are shown. Ignoring switches P & Q, track section 1 (see fig 150) is fed from controller A via busbar D, switch 1 and terminals 1 on terminal strips at control panel and baseboard (interconnected by cable). 'Common return' rail C is fed through terminals C and local busbar B. Similarly for sections 2 to 5. Section feeds always connect to switch ends of turnouts; never frog ends for reasons explained in fig 63. 1A is a dead end where to prevent trains hitting the buffers the end subsection is fed with reverse direction current *only* (a rectifier ensures this). Thus a locomotive stops on reaching the dead subsection but reverses out when the current flow reverses. 1B is a siding switched as a subsection of 1 so that locomotives may be parked there, in local control.

Sections 2-4 are simple but 5 contains four turnouts (all fed from their switch ends); this is logical as locomotives would not park on such a vital through section as this.

Section 6 has return loop RL where rail polarities can never be right at both ends of the loop simultaneously. No 'common return' is possible here; both loop rails must be isolated and switched. 6X & 6Y have separate, direct connections from controller A via double-pole switch Q, allowing travel round the loop in both directions. Switch P similarly allows travel in either direction in sections 1 to 5; having both switches allows trains to traverse the loop in either direction without stopping. Turnout 5T4 is set to the desired direction; for clockwise travel with all switches as drawn there will be correct correspondence of rail polarities, as indicated by red lamp R. When the train is on the loop both 5T4 and switch P are changed, extinguishing R and lighting green lamp G; rail polarities in sections 1 to 5 then correspond to those at the *lower* part of the loop and the train can run through 5T4 again without stopping.

Cab control is where an operator retains control of a train as it passes round a layout, instead of handing it over to another operator as it leaves a given section. To achieve this, each controller must be able to connect up to every running track section; but control of turnouts and signals may remain with the signalmen manning control panels around the layout. Thus the train operator is in the same situation as the driver of a real train. Whether the cab selects the sections or vice versa, interlocking is necessary to prevent two or more controllers being connected to the same section of track simultaneously. Portable or walkaround cab controllers enable the operator of a train to follow it around, plugging in to the nearest control panel at any time.

Electrical power may be provided in so many ways that it would take many volumes the size of this one to describe them all. The sketches and diagrams given in Appendix 2 bring out basic problems and typical solutions to them. For full understanding some knowledge of electricity is required, while far more sophisticated circuitry will be found in articles and books devoted exclusively to the subject.

Most model railways use direct current motors

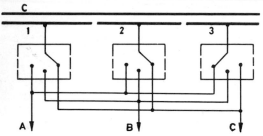

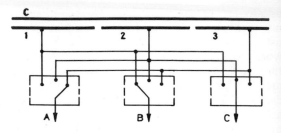

Fig 65 Cab control (local switching); Controller A is shown connected to track section 3 but cannot drive a train on to section 2 or 1 until 'signalmen' at local panels change their switches. As drawn, these are both set for controller C. In practice sections 1, 2 & 3 would represent numerous tracks electrically subdivided by local panel switches. (Upper C is common return rail, as in 64 & 66.)

Fig 66 Cab control (remote switching); Controller A is connected to track section 3; B to 1; and C to 2. But there is nothing to stop operators at controllers A and B trying to drive trains into section 2 while C is still in possession there. Without some form of electrical interlocking or overall control by a senior operator or 'dispatcher' issuing written 'train orders' it is best for the uninitiated to give this one a miss. It has advantages for operations of 'through' traffic on large layouts but local switching (fig 65) is better for local operations.

Fig 67 Partial cab control; Two separate operating areas W (white) and Y (yellow) can both be controlled by C1 if S1 is set in the position drawn. S2 takes care of rail polarities at interconnections having 'reverse loop' situations. With S1 in the other position C1 controls W and C2 controls Y. In other words, C2 controls the station, yards and roundhouse at Skunk River while C1 has the main line with its passing loops and sidings. Switches S1 and S2 can be seen below the ammeter in the centre of the control panel in fig 68.

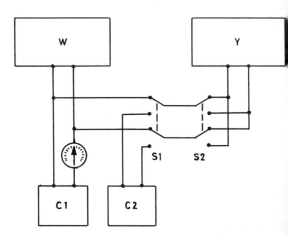

Fig 68 Control panel for yellow *(left)* and white *(right)* operating areas. Pushbuttons in 'tracks' on the mimic diagram control the turnouts; track section switches are in a long row across the top of the picture.

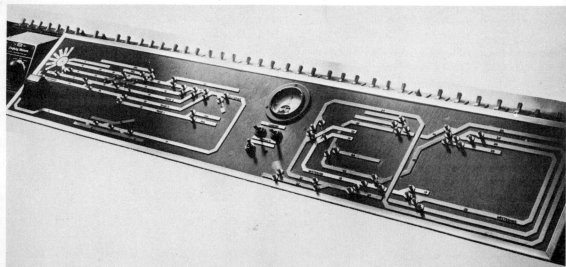

usually at 12 volts. One or two continental manufacturers though–Märklin in particular– use alternating current but the detail of how this works need not concern us here. It is important though to realise that while a low voltage ac model *might* work from direct current, they are designed from the start for ac control in association with various ac devices. In contrast, dc models must *never* be tried on ac. House mains must not under any circumstances be connected directly to *any* model or layout.

Transformers reduce mains voltage power to power at about 16–20V, which is safe for model railway use. For ac models and layouts it is only necessary to interpose a speed-controlling variable resistance, or rheostat, between transformer and track (with, of course, switches for isolating individual tracks, if several locomotives are in use). For dc models and layouts, though, a rectifier is also needed, to convert ac into dc; this is normally combined with transformer and rheostat in a totally-enclosed 'controller' provided commercially. Transformers and controllers are enclosed these days in heavy-gauge riveted casings, which it is dangerous for anyone other than a qualified electrician to remove. Properly-connected plugs and sockets with earth wires should be used.

Rheostats have the disadvantage of wasting power; when an engine is running downhill and drawing little current the power loss in the rheostat is small, but when it is working hard uphill and drawing a heavy current the loss in the rheostat is large. Therefore the engine tends to run away at top speed downhill and to slow or stall going up, at the same rheostat setting.

Instead of rheostats for speed control, it is possible to supply half-wave rectified ac at low speed-controller settings and to increase the amount of 'the other half' supplied until at full speed the output is *full*-wave. Appendix 2 should be consulted for more detailed explanations.

'Pulse power' is a similar concept, but here the increase in speed is achieved by increasing the width of successive square-shaped voltage pulses, usually employing electronic or solid-state circuits. Finally there is the variable transformer, which provides variable-voltage ac to the rectifier, making additional means of speed control unnecessary (although pulse power etc may still be incorporated in the same controller if desired). Well-designed and constructed model locomotives with sprung wheels and good-quality motors work very well from variable-transformer controllers, but others need pulse power to help avoid jerky starts. Pulse power produces noise and heat and should be used with care.

Small-size motors used in N and Z scales especially are easily overheated or burnt out, so special controllers with built-in high-resistance output circuits are required.

Silicon diodes, transistors, solid state and integral circuits are all used in modern power supply units or controllers. They are cheaper and lighter than the equivalent variable transformer units; they are more efficient; they react faster to changes in control settings; and they provide additional facilities such as increase or decrease of output power at rates which can be varied to give delayed slow, smooth starts and stops. Anything which happens gradually is dependent on charging or discharging a capacitor, and the overall time taken is varied by connecting resistors of different sizes in series with the capacitor; this is the simple basis of all simulated train momentum facilities, which ensure that no matter how fast the controls are turned from maximum to minimum or vice versa the train will slow down or speed up no faster than a real train weighing hundreds of tons.

Modern electronics and transistorised circuitry are fascinating studies, but we must resist the temptation to elaborate further; we have other bridges to cross!

CHAPTER SIX
CIVIL ENGINEERING

Bridges, tunnels, embankments and walls are needed wherever a railway line runs above or below the surrounding country, or crosses the route of another railway, a road or a waterway. Civil engineers try to adopt the least expensive route consistent with acceptable maximum gradients or minimum curvatures which might affect the weight and speed of trains.

They prefer to follow the contours of the land for country branch lines where traffic is light and infrequent, and to pick an economic alignment for main lines so that the amount of fill required for making embankments is just matched by the amount of soil and rock excavated from cuttings and tunnels.

Railways are often carried across city streets on lengthy viaducts because the land is valuable and embankments would take up too much room. Bridges are used to span stations, sidings and land earmarked for future development – often covered with rubbish dumps and signs reading '*This Valuable Building Site for Sale.*' If no other reason can be found to justify the use of a large bridge, this might do!

Modellers wishing to display a number of impressive bridges and other civil engineering works on their layouts must think the problems out in reverse; having decided on the desired structures, they proceed to arrange suitable obstacles for them to overcome. Harbours provide scope for swing and lift bridges; small ones in small harbours like Folkestone (69) and very large ones in some North American seaports and lake ports served by the St Lawrence Seaway. The bigger the bridge, the bigger the ships, cranes, warehouses, grain elevators etc which should appear in the background to give it moral support.

Gently undulating miniature landscapes lend themselves to economic alignments with a proper balance between excavation and fill but care should be taken to ensure that background scenery does not reveal an obviously easier route through the hills. Viewers are more likely to consider the railway route realistic if the background reveals an unbroken ridge of higher ground. In the ultimate a range of mountains, a winding, steep sided river gorge or a series of coastal cliffs forming a series of bays and headlands *compel* the use of major civil works and provide the modeller with ample justification for large-scale bridges and tunnels.

Fig 69 A BR up Continental Express crosses Folkestone Harbour swingbridge in the 1950s.
W. A. Corkill

Fig 70 Double-headed CPR Train No 3 (The Dominion; Toronto section, westbound) arrives at Whiskeyjack on the Mountain Subdivision as a long freight train (with five refrigerator cars; left foreground) waits in the passing loop.

Cross-country routes through the Pennines have their quotas of viaducts and tunnels while the main line from Dover plunges through a succession of tunnels in chalk cliffs which make magnificent background scenery. Between Koblenz and Trier in West Germany runs a very busy DB main line following the beautiful Mosel river gorge for many miles. At Bullay the river swings into a huge loop but the railway crosses over on a large double-deck bridge (79) and immediately tunnels under a ridge of the Eifel mountains. Beyond the south portal, the river reappears as the line climbs away on a long, low curved viaduct amongst the vineyards. All the above, not to mention Alpine pass routes and their North American equivalents, provide excellent prototype settings for civil works; distances must however be compressed and just one of the main spans of a big bridge like that at Bullay makes a fine model.

The choice of types of bridges etc is very wide, but there are some designs which have been superseded and should only be used on layouts of an appropriate era. The timber trestle was widely used in North America up to 1900, and on the GWR in England in the West Country in the same period, but about that time the increasing speed and weight of main line trains rendered it obsolete. Timber structures now survive only on a few backwoods branches and industrial lines. There is a British example at Barmouth in Wales but in Europe generally they are rare. Masonry viaducts, on the other hand, are more numerous in Europe than in North America. Some of the more common types of structures and details of their construction are set out below, and are illustrated in fig 71.

Suspension bridges A are best painted on the scenic background as they are only very rarely used for railways, lacking the stiffness to support modern trains.

Reinforced concrete arch bridges B are used to span moderately wide gorges; they are mostly of modern construction (since 1920) and at first sight they resemble masonry bridges having open spandrels (sides). They do not, however, have numerous courses of masonry and may be finished all over with a smooth, plain surface; this eases construction from wood or cardboard. Modern bridges like this since World War II are often of reinforced concrete, covered by stone facing to blend with the background.

Steel arch bridges C have been built since about 1890. They are mostly of complex girder construction which is difficult to model, and close attention to scale drawings or photographs is essential. As in B above, the weight of a train on the top deck is transferred to the lower arch, which in turn exerts horizontal as well as vertical loading on the rock at both ends of the structure.

Masonry arch bridges D with their massive pillars or abutments at the haunches (ends) of the structure are used for moderate to short spans, especially where the ground is too weak to withstand oblique loading from a true arch.

Continuous bridges E are invariably of steel construction, having one long girder each side, resting on end abutments such as R. Any number of intermediate support columns such as P and Q may be introduced to prevent excessive deflections and the whole of the steel part of the bridge is free to expand and contract with changes in temperature. It rests on bearing pads or rollers and *not* directly on masonry supports. The particular type shown is called a deck type continuous bridge because the railway line is carried on its upper surface, or deck.

Masonry viaducts F are used where the ground is firm and no great span is needed to bridge an obstacle. As shown, they are often used at the approaches to larger bridges in order to save cost. Bricks or stonework may be used, according to the locality.

Tunnel mouth G is a simple vertical or sloping wall of masonry or concrete with an oval or (sometimes) inverted U shaped aperture allowing clearances for the largest loads permitted on the line.

Retaining wall H, sometimes vertical but usually sloping at a small angle, or batter from the vertical, holds back earth or rock in the cutting sides which might spill over on to the track.

Culverts I are small square or elliptical tunnels (or pipes) allowing streams or drains to pass under embankments.

Beam bridges J consist of simple wooden, steel or concrete beams resting on masonry, timber or concrete abutments, often with retaining walls as shown. They present an easy way of bridging a gap not exceeding about 40 scale feet.

Through type plate girder bridges K are used for medium spans where clearances underneath are restricted; deck type bridges are always

TYPES OF CIVIL ENGINEERING STRUCTURES

Fig 71

cheaper to build than through type ones and are therefore used wherever clearances permit. The central girder must carry twice the weight carried by the two outer ones when two trains pass each other on the bridge, so it must be either half as tall again or of heavier section steel plate.

Deck type plate girder bridges L are easier to construct as only the outside faces of two girders are visible; all the interior parts may be simulated by a solid piece of wood. It would make little difference to the appearance of the structure shown if it consisted of one double-track or two single-track bridges, unless visitors could easily see the underside, which might then have to be accurately modelled.

Through type steel truss bridges M are used for spans of from 60 to 600 scale feet and are interesting and complex models in their own right. Excellent plastic kits by Faller, Vollmer, Kibri and other makers enable one to be assembled in a couple of evenings, but if the standard kit is unsuitable it is often possible to take parts from a number of kits and use them to build a bridge of different design. Some post-1945 bridges have parts made from welded box sections with no projecting webs, rivet heads or other projections and for these pieces of smooth, square or rectangular section obechi or balsa wood may be used. Similar construction may be used for reinforced concrete bridges but these should be finished in a pale grey or buff colour to simulate weathered concrete, instead of the usual darker grey for painted steelwork. The structure shown consists of two identical bridges side by side; but a single one having a central truss of heavier section parts could be used instead, or a single one having no central truss but taller or heavier outer trusses.

Abutments N, S, T and U are of different shapes according to the type of bridge(s) they carry, as will be obvious from the drawing. They may be solid wood, built up from wood or

longitudinal stringers carried on a series of vertical frames called bents. These are of two main types: pile bents driven into the ground, often without any form of diagonal bracing, and braced bents consisting of frames resting on the ground, on a flat rock surface or on masonry or concrete foundation plinths. The latter type of bent can usually be recognised by its lower mud-sills as well as by the diagonal bracing necessary to prevent it swaying in the wind or under the weight of a train. Some very

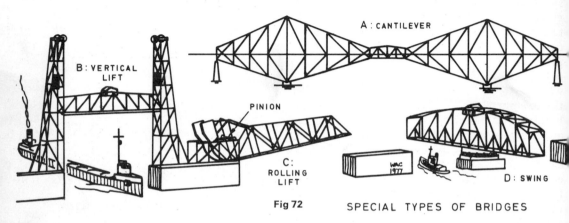

Fig 72   SPECIAL TYPES OF BRIDGES

cardboard sheet, or plastic kits with all the proper facing bricks or stones beautifully moulded in. Brick or stone paper, preferably the embossed type, may be stuck over plain abutments or they may be painted to resemble dirty concrete.

Late nineteenth-century steel trestle bridges W had trusses of zigzag or scissors (often called lattice) construction resting on light but complicated towers V. Stiff wires, brass sections or plastic kits may be used for these delicate dustcatchers.

Modern steel trestle bridges X are totally different and have plate girders of various types resting on towers whose bases are wide and well supported on concrete foundations. There are at the time of writing no kits or parts readily available but by studying drawings or photographs and using wire, knitting needles, parts of other bridge kits etc a fair representation can be made.

Timber trestles Z are used for temporary or industrial lines, especially in North America, where they were originally found on all main lines. The rails are spiked directly on to closely spaced crossties which are longer than the ties or sleepers on ordinary track and which rest on

nice timber or plastic kits are available, for timber trestles made by master joiners; in practice very haphazard work by contractors could sometimes be seen, or additional bracing was added when heavier trains appeared and the structure started to sag.

Refuges Y are familiar features of all long bridges, sometimes making room for one or two men to stand clear of a passing train and sometimes holding a red painted barrel of water in case of fire.

The above are all basic types of fixed structures; it would take a large layout to include one of each, and it is often better to combine several of the medium size ones (like K, L and M) than to try and squeeze in one big one.

Special types of bridges are shown in fig 72, all of which can be made to work by bridge-building enthusiasts having adequate time and skill.

Swing bridges D normally rest on a central pier with a substantial vertical shaft and collar or with a series of rollers resting on a surface plate; sometimes they have a longer arm stretching out over the water and a shorter but heavier arm swinging over the land. The difficulty is to make the free ends of the bridge (which is always a plate girder or steel truss type) line up accurately with the trackbeds on dry land; a sudden step which trains must run over is as bad as a bridge which reaches its final position with a sudden jerk. Electrical connections to the tracks can be through flexible wires or, if the bridge is arranged to rotate continuously when the driving motor is left running, a pair of slip rings or spring contact wipers will be needed.

Rolling lift or bascule bridges C pivot about one end and therefore take up less space than swing types. They require some knowledge of gearing and counterbalances and should not be tackled without actually seeing one in action or being able to study a good set of instructions provided with a kit.

Lift bridges B require smaller counterbalance weights and a set of pulley wheels in place of the complications of other lifting bridge types; both ends of the bridge must be lifted smoothly at the same rate for realistic operation. This is most easily achieved by means of a single electric motor driving a shaft with four drums, each of which winds up or lets out one of the four lifting wires through appropriately placed pulley wheels.

Cantilever bridges A are candidates for painting on the background, as they are rarely used for spans short enough to be found on most layouts. The main span at Quebec City is 1,800ft; of the Forth Bridge 1,710ft (twice) and of the Connell Ferry bridge (originally road and rail) near Oban in Western Scotland 524ft. These do not include approach spans which increase the overall length to over 3,000, 8,000 and 1,000ft respectively.

Steel plate bridge dimensions are given in fig 73. A typical through type side elevation is shown in A, a deck type side elevation in C and corresponding plan views in B and D. It is assumed

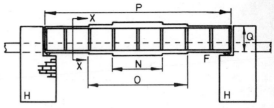

THROUGH TYPE-SIDE ELEVATION

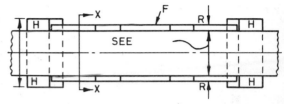

THROUGH TYPE-PLAN

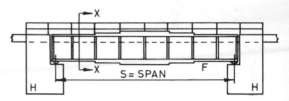

DECK TYPE – SIDE ELEVATION

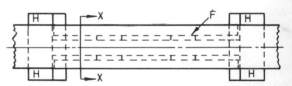

DECK TYPE – PLAN

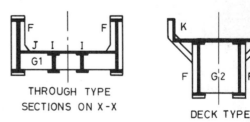

THROUGH TYPE
SECTIONS ON X-X

DECK TYPE

Fig 73 Plate girder bridge dimensions; The dimensions given are *average* figures for bridges of light/heavy construction; but bridges considered heavy in 1900 would be light by 1930 when heavy trains required more massive structures. Central girders between tracks, where used, are up to 50 per cent deeper and have one more cover plate than outside girders; they also have more intermediate stiffening angles. Alternatively, thicker plate may be used instead.

Spacing of angle sections varies but normally their distance apart is equal to or less than the beam depth, except on very light structures.

North American main lines use the heaviest bridges; branch lines and narrow-gauge railways the lightest. Most British and Continental main-line types are of medium weight.

Fig 73

Span(ft)	Dimensions(ft)				
	N	O	P	Q	R
30	–	–	32	3/6	1
50	–/20	20/30	53	3.8/6	1.25
70	–/30	45	74	4.5/8	1.5
90	–/40	55	94	6/9.3	1.75

that the trackbed in each case is a strip of wood which is continued right through the bridge; if the bridge is required to lift out because it spans a baseboard joint this will need to be modified. For very short spans the extra cover plates (of length N and O) may be omitted; for medium spans there is only one and for very long spans there may be three or four. The span is precisely defined as the distance between supports, not the length of the girders or the distance between feet of the abutments, H. Handrailing is shown in elevation C but in North America this is unusual; the only guard is a square section strip of wood across the ends of the crossties. Sections are shown in E, however, with a steel plate tray, K, to hold the ballast or to act as a guard. Rails are positioned in between girders F, which are cross-connected by diaphragm plates G2, and the weight of trains is transferred from the rails to the girders through timber crossties. In the through type, the girders are much further apart (to allow clearance to trains) and diaphragms G1 cannot take the weight of trains by themselves.

Longitudinal stringers I are therefore introduced and rails can be bolted directly on to them through the floorplates J (if any). Ballasted track may be used if trains are fast or if the bridge is otherwise susceptible to vibration; and this is much easier to model when using plastic-sleepered flexible track which can be mounted on preformed foam plastic underlay.

Plate girder bridge construction is shown in fig 74 for those wishing to make their own out of sheet plastic card or similar material, after practising with a few simple plastic kits. Sheet plastic card is cut by scribing with a sharp knife and then bending to cause shearing along the scribed lines. Parts are trimmed with a smooth file, checked with a straight edge and set square, and then tacked in position at the edges with small dabs of polystyrene cement. When this has set firmly, the joints are completed by running in a liquid solvent such as methyl ethyl ketone, with a fine paint brush. With a little practice it is possible to make a very firm joint with no trace of excess glue or cement. Large amounts of poly-

Fig 74 PLATE GIRDER BRIDGE CONSTRUCTION

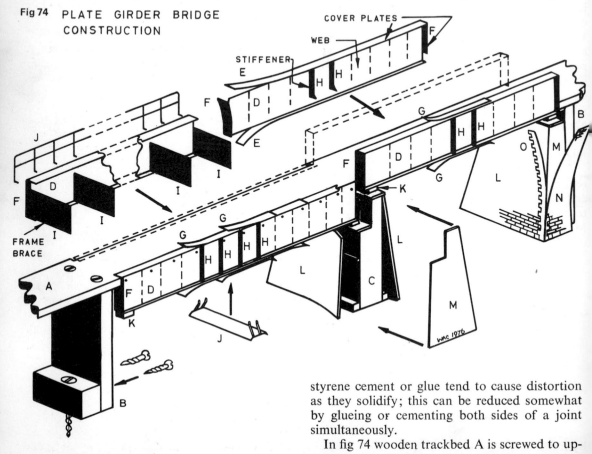

styrene cement or glue tend to cause distortion as they solidify; this can be reduced somewhat by glueing or cementing both sides of a joint simultaneously.

In fig 74 wooden trackbed A is screwed to up-

Fig 75 Very substantial bridges carried fast-moving, heavy loads like this red-panelled, gold-lined 87(HO)16.5 T-1-a Selkirk 2-10-4. A similar bridge crosses the Bear River.

rights B and C which in turn are firmly secured to the baseboard. Plate girders D may be identical but the trackbed is cut away to accommodate the left-hand pair. The web has top, bottom and end cover plates E and F and intermediate stiffeners H; the inside ones on the right-hand girders have small triangular gussets at the bottom. Underneath frame braces I may be pieces of card, X-shaped angle-iron bracing or solid wood. Extra cover plates G strengthen the girder in the middle, where it would be most highly stressed in their absence. Smoke baffle plates J are fitted over lines on which steam trains run; their exhaust might damage the paintwork of the girders.

All girders rest on cast iron bearings K which rest on abutments whose side walls are L and end walls are M. As the abutments slope inwards towards the top in all directions the true shape of M and N (for cutting out of card) cannot be obtained from front and side elevations (fig 76).

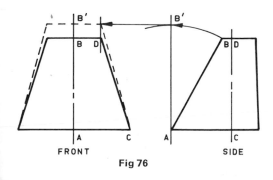

Fig 76

By rotating a side wall to the upright position so

that its top moves from B to B′ in the right-hand elevation we are able to draw a true view of it in the left-hand elevation. A similar construction is used to find the true shape of the end piece by moving D to D′ (not shown).

Abutments are covered with brick or stone-paper N, and quoining stones O. Handrails J are made from brass wire soldered in a simple wooden jig (fig 77) in which all wires are a tight sliding fit. The top rail is bent over to fit into the jig at A and B, after which other wires are added and joints are soldered in the order C, D, E, F, G, H, I, J, K. It is inadvisable to work from one

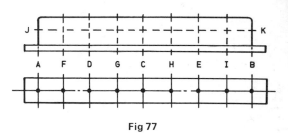

Fig 77

end towards the other; it is always better to start in the middle and divide the spaces successively. In this way, any errors in setting out dimensions are evenly distributed; this is standard practice in modelmaking.

Some popular types of trusses are shown in fig 78, with names of the principal components. The Warren can have subdivided panels to distribute the load on the deck which bears the weight of trains. A subdivided Pratt truss is called a Baltimore truss (or a Pennsylvania truss if the top chord is curved). Trusses always rest on bearings placed directly under the outer ends of chords or under intermediate posts; never under

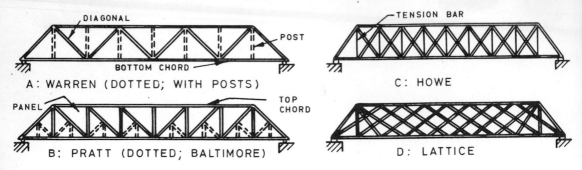

A: WARREN (DOTTED; WITH POSTS)

DIAGONAL

POST

BOTTOM CHORD

PANEL

B: PRATT (DOTTED; BALTIMORE)

TOP CHORD

C: HOWE

TENSION BAR

D: LATTICE

Fig 78 Some popular types of trusses.

a mid-panel. The support at one end is a hinge and at the other end a slider or roller to permit expansion.

The Howe truss was constructed of timber diagonals (in compression) with vertical iron tension bars. Diagonals were interlaced to make a fairly massive structure. The true lattice D used early forms of iron or steel angle-bars or rods to carry relatively light trains at low speeds. It would never do for heavy main line trains.

Fig 79 *(Above)* and 80 *(below)* An endless procession of heavy mineral trains crosses the double-deck DB bridge at Bullay. Short spans *(left)* fit a curve in the tracks above; the main span, simplified, makes a fine model. HO scale plastic kits were adapted to suit. The 85(HO)16.5 Fleischmann DB 2-10-0 pulls Liliput bogie hopper wagons.
W. A. Corkill; J. C. Coles

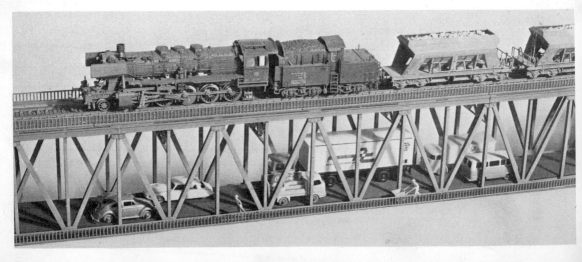

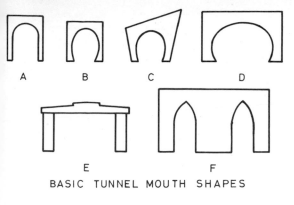

A   B   C   D

E   F

BASIC TUNNEL MOUTH SHAPES

Masonry shapes which are easily produced by the modeller are shown in fig 81 where A, B and C are single-track tunnel mouths; D, E and F two-track tunnel mouths. Shape A is more common in North America; B in Europe. E resembles types found along the Devon coast not far from Dawlish; F is found on the ex-SECR line at Shakespeare Cliff, Dover. Tunnels can have very ornate shapes but these are much more difficult to model. Tunnel-mouths G and H, of wood, thick card or linoleum (which can be carved to represent masonry courses) have wing walls I and supports J to hold them firmly in position. Curved liner K gives a solid appearance inside

TUNNEL :

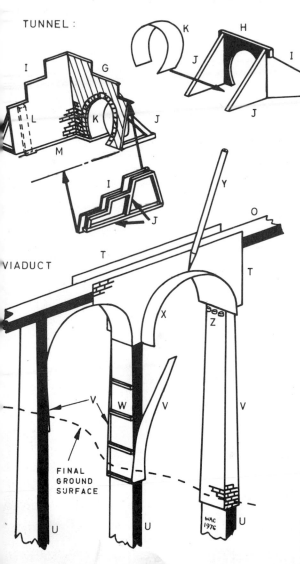

VIADUCT

FINAL GROUND SURFACE

UNDERBRIDGE :

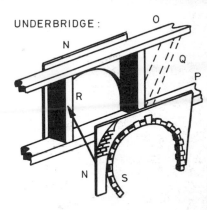

Fig 81 Masonry for modellers.

the tunnel, as far as can be seen from outside. L is a pilaster or buttress to strengthen a very big wall; M is the drainage ditch modellers often forget to provide, to conduct away rain-water and seepage. Underbridges and overbridges resemble tunnel-mouths, A. Sides N are fixed to trackbed O, carried off baseboard beam P by supports R. Keystone and quoining stones are separately purchased plastic spares by Faller or other makers, or are cut out of thin card. Viaducts are supported firmly from the baseboard structure at the foot of each column. Spandrels T are fixed to trackbed O and tops of columns U. Column sides and ends V are stuck on, using wood spacers W where necessary to maintain the correct angle of batter. The elliptical underside, or soffit, X, may be cut oversize and marked out with pencil Y as shown, especially if the viaduct is curved and on a rising gradient. Small projecting stones Z are sometimes used to support scaffolding for inspection and maintenance.

Avalanche shelters and galleries are often of masonry or concrete construction with windows or ports along one side. They may be made of wood faced with stone-paper or painted to resemble concrete; or they may be of plain or carved plaster. Switzerland, the Italian Riviera coast around Genoa, and the Rockies are places to find prototypes.

Turntables are special types of swing bridge whose weight may be supported at a central bearing, on end wheels running on a circular rail or track, or by a combination of both methods. Those having very large girders, built in the early 1900s, were supported on end wheels only; more modern ones with three-point suspension had much lighter girders.

British turntables were operated by hand or by a vacuum connection to the locomotive brake system; North American turntables had electric motor or compressed air drives housed in a small hut at one end of the bridge deck, Continental types had powerful air motors or diesel engines housed in large huts, and German types were rotated at astonishing speeds. Model turntable drives are by electric motor housed in the hut and turning the wheels through worm gears and a horizontal shaft, as in the 1960 vintage Fleischmann example at Skunk River/Aix photograph 20) or by slow-speed electric motor and gears turning a vertical central shaft projecting beneath the baseboard.

Electrical supplies to track and motor are picked up through slip rings, and the table may be aligned accurately with approach tracks by a locking bar which is withdrawn by a solenoid when the table is moving but which is allowed to engage with a hole in the pit wall when the desired track is reached. This action breaks the supply to the motor at the same time.

Traversers are bridges which move from side to side, and both ends are simultaneously locked in line with approach tracks; they are used in situations where there is insufficient space for turntables, as at the entrance to the electric locomotive depot at Mainz Hauptbahnhof in West Germany.

A: REGULAR COURSES

B: RANDOM COURSES

C: RANDOM STONEWORK

MASONRY PATTERNS

Fig 82

Fig 83 Rear of the Hawes Inn, South Queensferry, with Forth Bridge approach span.
W. A. Corkill

Fig 84 Hinge support at one end of an MSCR steel truss bridge at Trafford Park.
W. A. Corkill

CHAPTER SEVEN
SCENERY

Illustrations such as 70 and 87 must surely obviate the necessity for describing how scenery enhances a layout; but there are various types of scenery.

Simple infilling is shown in 91 where the basic medium is flat white undercoat paint; small quantities of this are decanted into jam jars and thinned with white spirit. To one jar are added lemon yellow and burnt sienna students' oil colours to make a sandy shade of paint suitable for paths, yards and waste land. A darker brown mix is used for ploughed land and bare earth; a light neutral green for grass and a dark bluish-grey for tarmac road surfaces.

When these base colours have been applied, and have dried, small spots and patches of a darker green to represent weeds, moss and ivy (on walls) are stippled on with the ends of hairs of a nearly dry brush, or rubbed across rough surfaces with a finger or thumb. Matt paints are best for scenery painting, but any shine may be removed from glossy surfaces by brushing on a thin coat of matt varnish.

After all paint and varnish has dried, watery glue may be brushed over areas to be covered with scatter material. This consists of short textile strands, sawdust or granulated cork dyed to resemble grass, earth, cornfields, heather, buttercups, poppies and so on.

Treated lichen from a model shop comes dyed in green or autumn tints and it should not be painted over; paint destroys its enduring natural softness and makes it dry up and crumble. Small pieces are planted with a dab of glue to represent bushes and hedgerows and larger ones can be propped against walls and rocks to look like larger bushes or young trees. Wire wool may also be pulled into the shape of hedges and bushes, but it will rust in damp atmospheres unless carefully painted.

Stone walls are made of balsa wood, plaster of Paris, modelling compounds or plastic materials; fences and gates are made from strips of card, wood or preformed plastic materials. Dyed felt or lint can be used to simulate grass fields or lawns, instead of scatter materials.

Almost any surface may be treated by the above methods; wood, hardboard, insulation board, preformed plastic layout mats etc. Small outcrops of rock are suggested by cork bark, whose rugged shapes may be carefully arranged to resemble deeply eroded strata. Spaces around and between pieces of cork bark are filled in with moist plaster, whose surface is roughed up before it sets hard.

Smooth areas of rock, soil or grass are simulated by pieces of canvas impregnated with varnish, by papier mâché (shredded newspaper mixed with flour and water, applied wet and allowed to harden) or by plaster (or proprietary fillers if not too expensive) spread on coarse textiles or paper layers with a small pointing

Fig 85 An uncompleted curved viaduct, which would look nice on the West Highland line. Rocks are of plaster and some trees were obtained from garden shrubs.

trowel. All these materials need support from chicken wire, wood formers or screwed-up newspaper, according to the area covered. Rocks, mountains and slopes in 70 and 85 were made from ordinary hardwall plaster from a hardware store. Chicken wire was stapled to timber supports attached to the baseboard and covered with pieces of coarse textile material cut from onion or carrot bags provided by a helpful greengrocer. Two or three layers of plaster reinforced with textiles make a strong surface but still more strength is obtained by adding a coarse mat of glass fibre, as used for repairing motor car bodies. Scenery can also be made from glass fibre-reinforced resin, which is very light and strong

but expensive and liable to give off pungent fumes when first applied. Its surface is smooth and needs sanding down, or rubbing with plaster when nearly dry.

A final plaster surface is smoothed over by hand to remove all sharp edges and trowel marks, and is roughened by rubbing with nearly dry plaster from the bottom of the mixing pan.

Finishing off, after painting, involves planting out bushes and trees, the best of which are placed prominently in the foreground and the least attractive ones further to the rear. Backgrounds are left free from vegetation (or shadows cast by it) in order to preserve illusions of distance or perspective (ie diminution of size with distance).

Perspective in 53 is used to suggest a width of a mile or more in the lake, although in practice it is only inches wide. The illusion is helped by painting the lake surface on a board tilted at 45 degrees so that its apparent width remains constant from almost every normal viewing distance. Rock formations around the far ends of the lake have blue-grey tones which merge with the mountain background; it is difficult to decide where the background scene really begins.

Background mountains and hills have vague, general outlines and subtly changing pastel colours with no sharp detail to attract the eye and destroy illusions of distance. Plaster smeared on the wall or backdrop board can help to give a bit of body to mountains, whose rugged strength contrasts strongly with delicate white clouds drifting past on the breeze.

Scenery for portable layouts must be light, so ordinary plaster is unsuitable. Instead, finer textiles or cotton bandages are soaked in wet plaster of Paris and applied in layers over crumpled newspaper to form a strong, light hard shell. Specially prepared scenic modelling kits are available, which are useful for small areas but expensive for large ones.

Trees are made from plastic kits, raffia or string trapped in twisted wires, or lichen glued lightly to dead twigs or roots of garden shrubs. Lichen naturally resembles deciduous trees in full leaf, but raffia or string may need filling out with glued sawdust and dyeing or painting in various shades of green to represent larch, spruce, pine or fir. Chicken feathers can be used for palm tree fronds.

Fig 86 A 148(N)9 BR electric train shoots out of Rabbit Warren Tunnel into the sunshine.

Fig 87 It is alleged that lawyer McWheedle acquired his Kiltiecrankie mine in lieu of litigation fees. The 76(OO)16.5 'Inverness Mail' will pass directly above gunpowder barrels stored under the arch!

The cheapest and most prolific source of trees is the garden; seed spikes of spiraea make poplars, those of buddleia make tall pines and spruces, and the umbelliferous heads of achillaea or yarrow make stone pines or, with a bit of modification, scots firs. The shapes may not be exactly right, but groups and groves have a live appearance; even a windswept one. The treatment for spikes is to let them dry for a week, then dip in glycerine or linseed oil and hang up to drip dry. Afterwards, paint to desired shades and plant out!

Water is represented by flat, glossy surfaces or by transparent glass (plain or dimpled) or layers of perspex or transparent paper through which can be seen water weeds, old motor car bodies, iron bedsteads or bicycle frames resting on a muddy bottom. Cascades and rapids are best viewed from a distance as irregular streaks and patches of white paint on a dark background.

Seascapes present a problem with ends of backdrops showing the horizon; a sudden sharp vertical edge in mid-ocean is *so* disturbing! Cliffs or headlands at either side are useful here, or tall warehouses and grain elevators can be positioned where they block the view of awkward spots.

City scenes look complicated but only low foreground buildings (such as parcels sheds) need be modelled, and even they can be in low relief (ie only the front half is modelled, and it rests against the backdrop). Taller buildings, which in Montreal for example are all quite different in design, finish and colouring, can be drawn and painted on the backdrop with a minimum of detail.

Towns and villages are best represented by a few buildings in 'Station Road' (91) and by a painted or printed backdrop suggesting the presence of others further back. There is no need

to crowd in the whole village, especially if there is plenty of vacant development land nearby.

Industrial scenes may occupy too much space for modelling, but a steelworks would make a splendid background to some industrial sidings. Sawmills are easier to model, and one can see logs go in at one end and planks come out at the other, giving cause for two types of train loads. Mines and quarries have storage hoppers, slag heaps, big corrugated iron or wooden sheds housing machinery and boilers, and junk lying about the place. Almost any large shed can look like a factory if adorned with roof ventilators, pipes and a chimney or two. The products made there may be openly displayed, or a closely guarded secret protected with security fences and police dogs.

Most industrial plants make interesting backgrounds but it is advisable to take a really close look before modelling one, or to seek expert advice. It just is not done to display mines without winding gear or power stations with coal handling plant but no chimneys!

Fig 88 Peter Moore used solid wood platforms, printed card buildings and plastic components in his Selhurst terminus, seen under construction. Note the 'push-and-pull' train and milk tank wagons.

Fig 89 Downtown Montreal with freight sheds and a 'French-Canadian' boxcar.
W. A. Corkill

CHAPTER EIGHT

REAL ESTATE

Buildings and off-line structures differ from civil works previously described, in detail; they need not support the weight of trains. They are available in the form of plastic or card kits in vast profusion. Serious students of railway and lineside architecture may contemplate drawing and constructing their own buildings, but they tend to specialise in a particular era or railway. A brief general survey will therefore be more appropriate than detailed descriptions.

British station platforms are much higher than Continental or North American ones; and at Wabamun (90) there is nothing but a small patch of planking for passengers to alight on. Shortly after this picture was taken, the CNR Super-Continental (three big diesels and 18 passenger cars) flashed past with a blare of horns and a cloud of dust. So much for Wabamun! Higher platforms make British station arrangements rather more formal than those at Whiskeyjack, where a road passes right through the middle of the station (70) and a series of common types is shown in 92. These include side platforms, island platforms, both on, above and below street level. Extra platforms and tracks

may of course be added to these basic forms to make up stations of any desired size.

Station buildings are shown in illustrations, made of printed card and plastic materials. Both are equally effective as typical buildings and they can be added to or modified to fit any particular layout or scheme. If, however, buildings are

Fig 90 Wabamun station beside the CNR main line in Alberta. *W. A. Corkill*

Fig 91 A Grafar GER 148(N)9 0-6-0T runs round its train at Bishop's Stratford. The station and terraced houses *(left)* are of printed card; the goods shed and hopper were plastic kits.

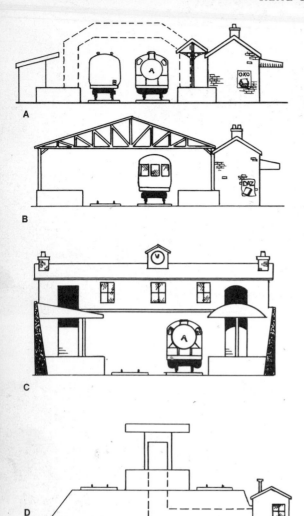

however, fit into window spaces from the inside; roofs must therefore be left off until all windows and doors have been fitted and secured with a minimum amount of glue, polystyrene cement or (in plastic card walls) of methyl ethyl ketone. Buildings containing working electric lights need to have detachable roofs, or to be detachable themselves from the baseboard for maintenance or repairs.

Fig 93A Simplicity in the ex-GER station house at Newport. *W. A. Corkill*

Fig 92 British station types: A-station house *(right)* and simple shelter *(left)*, with footbridge dotted. B-overall station roof. C-overhead station building with shelters and stairs D-island platform on embankment with stairs to low-level station house.

Fig 93B Elegance on Newport's up-line platform, seen from the footbridge. *W. A. Corkill*

made from scratch the sides and roofs are cut from sheets of cardboard, strawboard, wood or plastic card, often with a second set of inner walls having slightly oversize window spaces. Squares of mica or transparent plastic materials are trapped in between the inner and outer walls to represent window glass, and window panes are made from very thin, narrow strips of card. Some plastic kit suppliers sell windows separately as spares and if these are the right size they speed up construction. They usually,

Fig 94 *(upper)* and **96** *(lower).* Two stations with freight sheds attached: the attractive half-timbered DB station at Hatzenport/Mosel and timber-built HO scale Whiskeyjack station with the local sawmill. Note a TH&B gondola full of sawn lumber; log cars; CPR baggage and express car (at the station); auto rack car, boxcar (with hoboes), cattle car, gondola, hopper car and caboose (upper line, rear).
W. A. Corkill; J. C. Coles

Fig 95 The station and village at St Jodok/Brenner in Austria.
W. A. Corkill

Locomotive depots are illustrated in severa(l)
pictures. There is a simple engine shed in 98
approached by straight tracks as in 23H and the
roundhouse type appears in 34. For both basic
types there are wide variations.

Coaling arrangements include a simple hand
operated crane lifting buckets or wheeled skips
of coal from a wagon or coal-heap to the locomotive's tender or coal bunker (99C); a similar
type where wheeled skips are tipped from an
overhead stage; a raised shed, approached by
a steep ramp up which coal wagons are pushed
or winched, with openings at one side through
which coal is shovelled into locomotives' tenders
(99B), and very tall plant in which coal is lifted
to the top of a bunker holding perhaps 400 tons
or more. In British reinforced concrete types
(97) a coal wagon standing on a movable
track was lifted to the top of the structure and
bodily tipped over to discharge its load, while

Fig 97 LMS coaling plant and ashpits at Carnforth (Steamtown).
W. A. Corkhill

Fig 98 SR 76(OO)16.5 N15 4-6-0 No 796 *Sir Dodinas Le
Savage* on turntable between engine shed *(left)* and goods
shed (roof removed for access to turnout solenoids) a(t)
Selhurst.

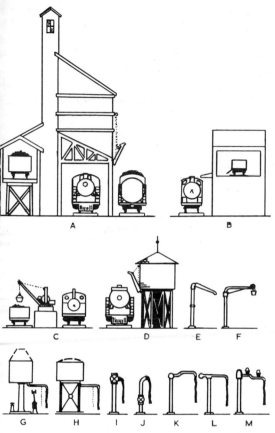

Fig 99 Locomotive facilities: A-North American coaling tower. B-British coaling stage (water tank above). C-Continental coaling crane with skips. D, E, F-N American water tower, water spout, oil column (with drip bucket). G to L-British water tanks and columns. M-German water column with red lamps.

in North American timber-built ones (99A) or reinforced concrete ones coal was discharged from hopper cars into a chamber from which skips conveyed it to the top of the bunker. Locomotives alongside or underneath were coaled by chutes lowered to the tender. Some very large timber examples were built which were masterpieces of joinery; sometimes they straddled main lines so that locomotives on fast trains could stop to take on ten tons of coal in two minutes, or less.

Ash disposal from steam locomotives was by dumping on the track or into pits between the rails (97) after which it was shovelled by hand into wagons, or into skips which were lifted by crane for tipping into wagons on an adjacent track or by hoist into an overhead bunker or discharge point for loading into wagons below. There is a good example of the latter type at Steamtown, Carnforth.

Sand for steam locomotives was dried in small buildings with chimneys, and conveyed by over-

Fig 100 (left) LMS water column at Carnforth (Steamtown). W. A. Corkill
Fig 101 (above) BR No 8 Llywelyn taking water on the Vale of Rheidol line at Aberystwyth. British Rail

Fig 102 Kentsford signal box on the ex-GWR Minehead branch.
W. A. Corkill

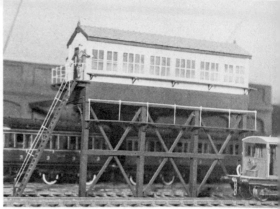

Fig 103 Ex-LNWR gauge O overhead signal box and brake van *(right)* at Bridgewater.
J. Brown

head pipe to a separate compartment in some North American coaling towers, and still is taken to overhead bins or hoppers for diesels.

Water tanks were usually cylindrical vessels supported on a central pillar in Britain or on steel or timber frames in North America, while Continental lines favoured brick or reinforced concrete towers. Water columns, cranes, hydrants (call them what you will) remote from tanks or towers were of very numerous designs, each British railway having its own ideas. Continental types often carried lamps showing a red light when the arm fouled the tracks and North American ones had a distinctive type of spout. Similar ones for supplying oil had a bucket hanging at the end to catch the drips and those which supply oil for diesel locomotives have flexible hoses.

Goods depots or freight sheds were often attached to the main station in North America, but in Europe a separate building was more common.

Signalboxes (called interlocking towers in North America) vary from small ground level huts with windows giving a good view of the track to large, tall structures like the bridge tower of a major warship, as at Frankfurt and Munich in West Germany. Modern British ones are long, two or three storey buildings with flat, featureless roofs; but Victorian examples were often delightful examples of good taste and architectural

interest. Some views of older boxes are shown in 102 and 128. Lack of space never deterred signal engineers, who perched boxes on walls, columns or frames spanning the tracks 103. Continental types were often solid, brick-built structures with tiled roofs and overhanging eaves; alternatively the signal controls were installed in a room in the station house, thus obviating the need for a separate building. North American towers were few and far between, found only at approaches to major junctions or terminals. Intermediate stations had train order signals (see Chapter 9) operated by controls installed inside the station house, or depot; in the steam era the Wabamun depot sported a set of train order signals above the bay windows.

Electrical catenary cables, wires and masts are one type of overheads that *can* participate in model train operation, by supplying current to locomotives and railcars. Contact wires, from which current is collected by pantographs on high speed services or trolley poles (on trams or inter-urban railways), are stretched taut by

Fig 104 GWR No 4983 *Albert Hall* negotiates a turnout whose operating solenoid is cunningly hidden beneath a platelayers' hut. The 'rocks' are cork bark.

Fig 105 *(above)* Aix-Les-Bonnes electrified: it's washday at the *cheminots'* canteen (a pensioned-off *fourgon*) as a Jouef *SNCF* 87(HO)16.5 four-pantograph Co-Co electric locomotive passes with the Indirect Orient.

Fig 106 N scale 'catenary' masts at Rabbit Warren Tunnel; a brass one with tensioning weight and pulley *(right)* and a Vollmer plastic one *(left)*.

weights suspended from masts at regular intervals. They are supported from cables hanging in a natural curve called a catenary, by numerous short links seen in 106. Some light railway or inter-urban systems have contact wires only, in which case the masts or wooden poles must be close together. Ready-made model catenary, as the whole apparatus is colloquially called, comes soldered together and plated over, ready for instant use; suppliers of common varieties include Sommerfeldt and Vollmer, and French and Swiss model shops have a very wide variety of native types. Kleinbahn, of Austria, make catenary stamped out of hard copper sheet; this can easily be cut, soldered or painted as it is supplied in bare metal. It has been used for the scene in 105.

Masts of common types for supporting 25kV ac wires (France and Britain) or 15kV ac wires (Germany, Switzerland, Austria) are shown in 106. When three or more tracks were spanned, early schemes used massive overhead gantries; more recently, the system using tall masts supporting transverse catenaries has become more widely used. Italian railways, however, have their own distinctive type of masts constructed from tubular steelwork. On all ac systems, power cables from substations are fed in at regular intervals and there are neutral sections where contact wires can be switched on or off, or connected to alternative supplies. Duplicate wiring and sets of insulators are required at these points. Home built contact wires and catenaries as distinct from the preformed ready-made commercial lengths can be tensioned by springs mounted inside tunnels or overbridges, or by fixing masts round the outside of track curves at a slight angle to the vertical. These are pulled upright by the wires, which must not be allowed to slacken off and become entangled with adjacent signals.

CHAPTER NINE

SIGNALS AND AUTOMATIC CONTROLS

Chapter Five with Appendix 2 described methods of controlling electrically driven trains, but now it is time to introduce signals which trains obey (or appear to obey) as they move from station to station round the layout. Many modellers operate their layouts without them altogether; others introduce full interlocking and automation with panels full of relays and electronic devices.

Signals on real railways indicate 'stop', 'proceed' or 'proceed with various restrictions as to speed or direction', and differences arise mainly with the last-named. On railways throughout the world the basic application of signalling is to show train drivers approaching a station or junction either which route they are to take, or the speed at which they may travel, or whether they must stop at or before the station or junction. Trains cannot stop quickly from high speed and must therefore have advance warning of the indications of signals ahead. Thus railway signals are generally grouped into three types – those that give advance indications of the state of signals ahead, called distant signals in Britain; signals allowing entry to a station or approach to a junction, usually called home signals in Britain but entry signals in Europe; and signals authorising moves out of a station or away from a junction into the block section ahead, usually called starting signals in Britain but exit signals in Europe. The home and starting signals in Britain are of the same pattern, called stop signals, in that when at danger they require a train to stop at them. Sometimes at complicated stations or junctions a distant signal applying to the starting signal is placed underneath the home signal. This is often the practice in Europe even when the station is controlled by one signalbox but in Britain is only used when the signals at each end of the station are worked by two (or more) signalboxes. The distant signal is of course controlled by the same signalbox as the stop signals to which it applies. Thus where we have a stop signal above a distant signal (fig 108A) the stop signal would be controlled by one signalbox and the distant by the next box ahead.

Many of the various types of signal are available commercially and sometimes not only in their country of origin. In Britain sometimes you can obtain German and Swiss signals as well as British types. Most are, or can be arranged, for electric operation.

British semaphores are grouped so as to show drivers which route they will take, and they are expected to know the speed restrictions involved in doing so. The most important route is indicated by the tallest signal 'doll' on a bracket or gantry (fig 109, B1 and B2) and secondary routes by shorter dolls. French signals may be grouped with speed restriction signals which are clear (unseen) if the route is set for the main line over which there is no restriction, and are displayed only when the route is set for the lower-speed divergence (fig 115). Indeed most French mechanical signals are boards or discs, face-on to the driver for danger or caution, and edge-on (and virtually unseen) for clear. German semaphores

Fig 107 A Ratio plastic GWR signal shows 'proceed' for the 8.56am (SO) Ramsgate to Birkenhead (Train No 970 in ex-GWR territory) whose two white lamps indicate 'express passenger train'.

are often grouped to indicate speed restrictions, regardless of route (fig 116, D1), and North American signals can have up to four arms mounted on a single post to indicate all manner of routes and speed restrictions (fig 119A).

In each case, the illustration shows groups of signal arms where at times there may be only one; the idea is to enable meanings of grouped

dotted. British stop signal arms are painted red with a white vertical stripe near the left hand end. Brackets similar to junction signal B but with dolls of equal height can be found at each end of large stations where all tracks have equal importance. Small signal arms C or discs D control shunting movements either in stations and yards or access to main running lines beyond yard

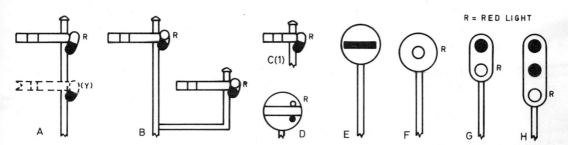

Fig 108 British 'stop' signal indications: A to E are semaphores; F is a searchlight signal; G and H are 2- and 3-aspect colour-light signals.

signals to be understood (at least in general terms) when encountered in modelling a prototype situation. Corresponding indications of simple colour-light signals are also given. Additional indications are given by some colour lights but for most model railway purposes the signals shown in the diagrams will be adequate. On modern main lines, with few intermediate stations, sections are divided by colour light signals normally worked automatically by trains themselves, but few model lines have the space

limits. Banner repeater signals E are placed before bridges or other obstructions which prevent timely sighting of stop signals, but trains are not required to stop at a repeater signal itself.

The 'proceed' indications of British stop signals are shown in fig 109. Upper and lower quadrant arms have the same meanings; somersault types formerly used on the GNR and LNER are lower quadrant type variations. Ex-GWR lines still use lower quadrant signals (107) but elsewhere they are less common.

British 'caution' signal indications are shown in 110. Signal B3 warns that the junction signal which it precedes is at stop, whereas B4 advises

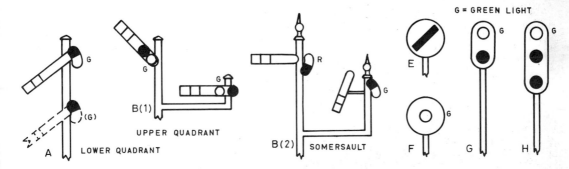

Fig 109 British 'proceed' signal indications: B(1) indicates 'proceed on direct route'; B(2) indicates 'proceed on route diverging to the right'.

for long lengths of plain line like this.

British stop signal indications are shown in fig 108, where A has the same meaning with or without a second (fishtailed-distant) arm shown

that the junction signal ahead is set for 'proceed via diverging line to the right'. Distant signals, which are painted yellow with a black chevron near the left hand end, always precede a group of stop signals. When signals are closely spaced (as on most layouts) home and distant arms are often placed together as in A, B3 or B4 above.

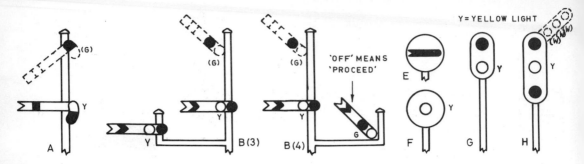

Fig 110 British 'caution' signal indications: the vertical stripe on the distant signal was in use until the 1920s on some railways; H is shown with optional (dotted) route indicator, warning of a divergence to the right when lit.

British shunt signal indications, shown in 111, have numerous variations but those shown are the most common. Ringed signals had the meanings shown in I. They were not shunting signals

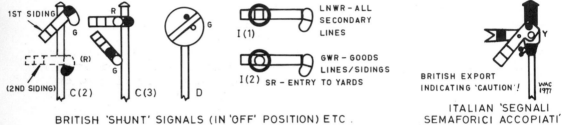

BRITISH 'SHUNT' SIGNALS (IN 'OFF' POSITION) ETC.

Fig 111

ITALIAN 'SEGNALI SEMAFORICI ACCOPIATI'

Fig 112

but were used on running lines on some railways.

Signals at Brakewell (a typical junction) are shown in fig 113 with thick arrows to represent trains. Note which signals are 'off' for a through train from Umbergate (upper sketch) and for a train leaving the bay platform at Brakewell. A, B, C, D, F, H and I are simple 'stop' and 'distant' examples, but E is the distant signal preceding the 'stop' arm of F and the junction signal G. According to which arm of G is clear, F can indicate 'signals ahead clear for main line to Umbergate' (E1) or 'next signals ahead clear for Bishop's Stratford branch' (E2). Italian semaphores are of British origin, but combined stop and distant signals usually have the arrangement shown in fig 112, which corresponds to 110A. Other continental signals are shown in 114 and 116, with indications given by the more common types. There are many more besides these, for which reference may be made to specialised works.

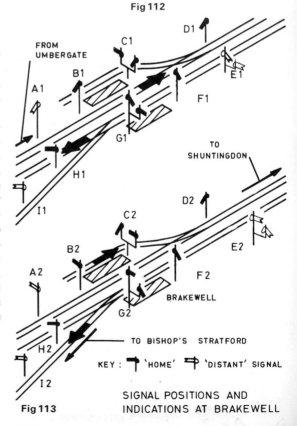

KEY: ↑ 'HOME'   ↗ 'DISTANT' SIGNAL

SIGNAL POSITIONS AND INDICATIONS AT BRAKEWELL

Fig 113

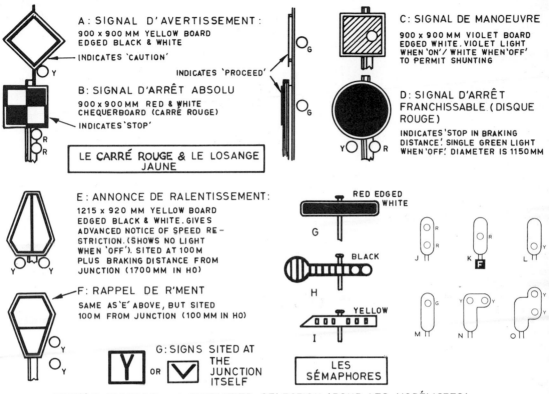

A: SIGNAL D'AVERTISSEMENT:
900 x 900 MM YELLOW BOARD
EDGED BLACK & WHITE
← INDICATES 'CAUTION'

INDICATES 'PROCEED'

B: SIGNAL D'ARRÊT ABSOLU
900x900MM RED & WHITE
CHEQUERBOARD (CARRÉ ROUGE)
← INDICATES 'STOP'

LE CARRÉ ROUGE & LE LOSANGE JAUNE

C: SIGNAL DE MANOEUVRE
900 x 900 MM VIOLET BOARD
EDGED WHITE. VIOLET LIGHT
WHEN 'ON' / WHITE WHEN 'OFF'
TO PERMIT SHUNTING

D: SIGNAL D'ARRÊT FRANCHISSABLE. (DISQUE ROUGE)
INDICATES 'STOP IN BRAKING
DISTANCE'. SINGLE GREEN LIGHT
WHEN 'OFF'. DIAMETER IS 1150MM

E: ANNONCE DE RALENTISSEMENT:
1215 x 920 MM YELLOW BOARD
EDGED BLACK & WHITE. GIVES
ADVANCED NOTICE OF SPEED RE-
STRICTION. (SHOWS NO LIGHT
WHEN 'OFF'). SITED AT 100M
PLUS BRAKING DISTANCE FROM
JUNCTION (1700 MM IN HO)

F: RAPPEL DE R'MENT
SAME AS 'E' ABOVE, BUT SITED
100M FROM JUNCTION (100 MM IN HO)

G: SIGNS SITED AT THE JUNCTION ITSELF

RED EDGED WHITE

G

BLACK

H

YELLOW

I

LES SÉMAPHORES

J   K   L

M   N   O

FRENCH SIGNALS — A SIMPLIFIED SELECTION 'POUR LES MODÉLISTES'

Fig 114 Colour-light signal K corresponds to a semaphore signal and may be passed at danger in certain circumstances.

French signalling has three different yellow signals. To understand why it is necessary to look at fig 115, where all signals are shown clear for a train going from Aix to Bourg. Here, A is the *disque rouge* (which if face-on to a train means stop before reaching the station – in this case before reaching the siding points approaching the station), B is a *losange jaune* type of *avertissement* with the *ralentissement* above; it is the 'distant' for *carré rouge* C, which has the *rappel*

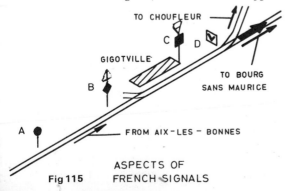

TO CHOUFLEUR

GIGOTVILLE

TO BOURG SANS MAURICE

FROM AIX - LES - BONNES

Fig 115 ASPECTS OF FRENCH SIGNALS

above it, while *chevron* D is placed at the junction itself. Had the route been set for a train diverging to the Choufleur line (with a speed restriction over the turnout) the *ralentissement* and *rappel* would have been face on to the driver.

In fig 114 semaphores G and H are both stop signals (but not absolute stop). In France a semaphore stop signal (showing one red light at night) can be passed at danger with the train proceeding at caution, in certain circumstances, after the train has first come to a halt. If a train must stop and not proceed until the signal clears (as at a junction) a *carré* is used instead (two red lights at night). I is a semaphore distant or *avertissement*, and has the same meaning as A. Semaphore distant signals are a relic from the old Nord system in Northern France. French colour-light signals usually correspond to night time mechanical indications. Some examples are shown in fig 114 J-O.

German standard signals, fig 116, are shown systematically, with the stop or *Hauptsignal* in the top row with the corresponding colour-light or *Tageslicht-signal* alongside; the preceding distant or *Vorsignal* is below, and the corresponding

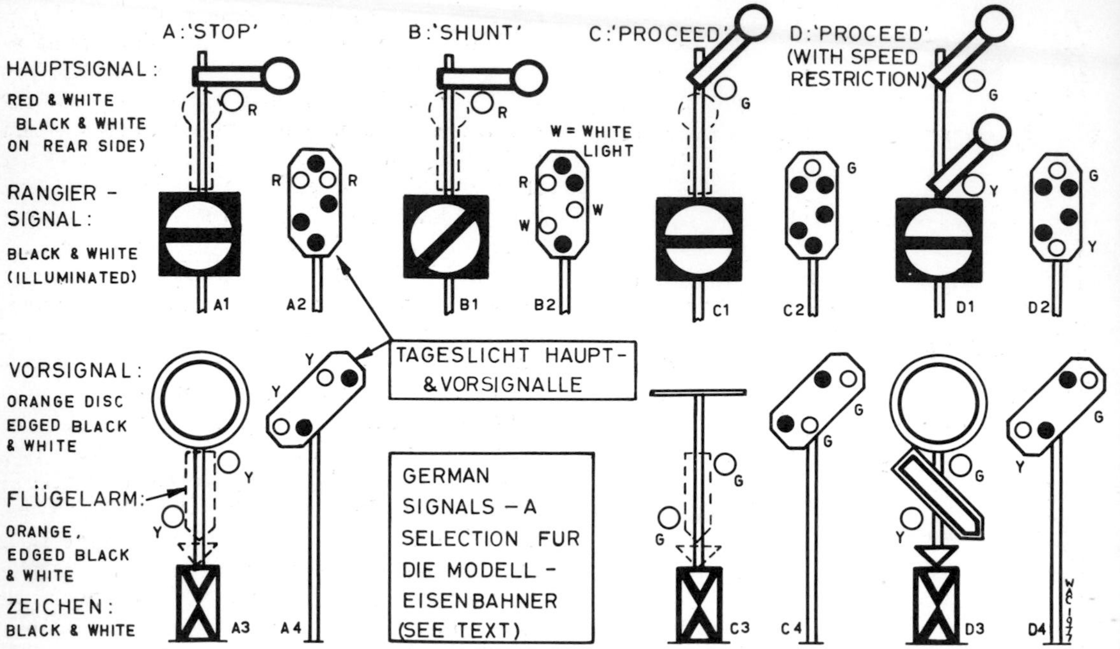
A:'STOP'
B:'SHUNT'
C:'PROCEED'
D:'PROCEED' (WITH SPEED RESTRICTION)
HAUPTSIGNAL:
RED & WHITE
BLACK & WHITE
ON REAR SIDE)
RANGIER - SIGNAL:
BLACK & WHITE
(ILLUMINATED)
W = WHITE LIGHT
R
G
Y
W
A1
A2
B1
B2
C1
C2
D1
D2
TAGESLICHT HAUPT- & VORSIGNALLE
VORSIGNAL:
ORANGE DISC
EDGED BLACK
& WHITE
FLÜGELARM:
ORANGE,
EDGED BLACK
& WHITE
ZEICHEN:
BLACK & WHITE
GERMAN SIGNALS - A SELECTION FUR DIE MODELL - EISENBAHNER (SEE TEXT)
A3
A4
C3
C4
D3
D4

Fig 116

Tageslichtvorsignal (colour-light distant) alongside. A shunting or *Rangiersignal* is shown in front of the *Hauptsignal*; there is no distant signal for this. Only in D1 has the second semaphore arm any part to play; similarly with D3 distant indication. These indicate that the route is set to a low speed route diverging from the main line. D1 would also be used to signal a train over a low speed route *to* the main line. All the signals shown may be found grouped together. Sometimes the *Rangiersignal* is cleared with the main semaphore arms. In Eastern France you can find German and French signals together sometimes at the same location, a relic of the last century when Alsace and Lorraine were part of Germany.

In fig 117 three countdown warning boards or *Barken* (*mirlitons* in French) are placed 250, 150 and 50m in front of a *Vorsignal* (B grouped with *Hauptsignal* C, or G grouped with H). *Doppel-*

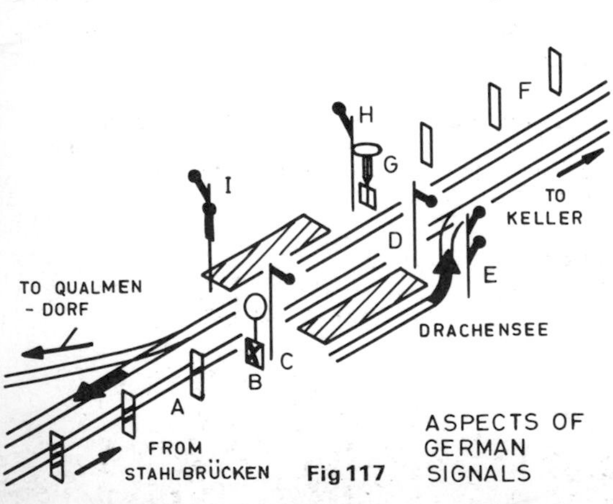
TO QUALMEN - DORF
FROM STAHLBRÜCKEN
TO KELLER
DRACHENSEE
A
B
C
D
E
F
G
H
I
ASPECTS OF GERMAN SIGNALS

Fig 117

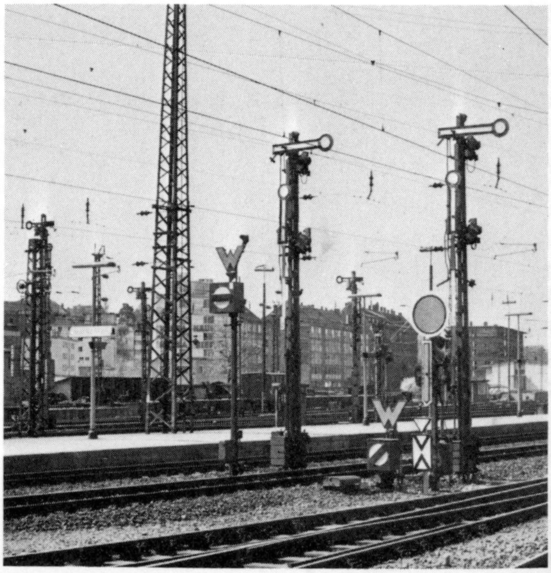

Fig 118 DB semaphore signals at Mainz *Hauptbahnhof*, under electrical 'catenary' wires.
W. A. Corkill

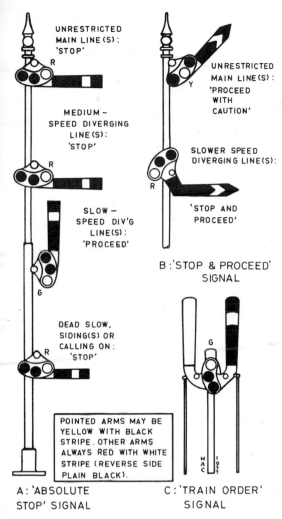

UNRESTRICTED
MAIN LINE (S):
'STOP'

R

MEDIUM –
SPEED DIVERGING
LINE (S):
'STOP'

R

SLOW –
SPEED DIV'G
LINE (S):
'PROCEED'

G

DEAD SLOW,
SIDING(S) OR
CALLING ON:
'STOP'

R

UNRESTRICTED
MAIN LINE (S):
'PROCEED
WITH
CAUTION'

Y

SLOWER SPEED
DIVERGING LINE(S):

R

'STOP AND
PROCEED'

B : 'STOP & PROCEED'
SIGNAL

G

POINTED ARMS MAY BE
YELLOW WITH BLACK
STRIPE. OTHER ARMS
ALWAYS RED WITH WHITE
STRIPE (REVERSE SIDE
PLAIN BLACK).

A : 'ABSOLUTE
STOP' SIGNAL

C : 'TRAIN ORDER'
SIGNAL

N. AMERICAN SEMAPHORE SIGNALS
DRAWN APPROX. TO 1:87 HO SCALE)

Fig 119 Signal C shows 'Proceed; no orders' to both east-
and westbound trains. See also fig 19, where an eastbound
is 'slowing to pick up a train order' (attached to a bamboo
hoop caught by the fireman).

flügelhauptsignal I indicates 'proceed' for a train
going to Stahlbrücken; had it been taking the
Qualmendorf line the speed restriction over the
turnout would have called for the same indication as that given by E. Signal E, however, can
give no other clear indication on account of the
reverse curve, while D can only give 'proceed'
or 'stop'.

North American signals are shown in fig 119,
the most widely used being train order signals
fig 119C. These can be left permanently at 'proceed; no orders' or 'slow for orders' without

affecting train operation in any way. Block signals are often 'permissive', allowing trains to
stop, wait a short while and then proceed at very
slow speeds. This is because signal failures might
halt trains indefinitely in remote locations, which
is highly undesirable in winter conditions. A
study of railroad rulebooks will show how much
detailed local knowledge is necessary for proper
understanding of differences between 'station',
'interlocking' and 'block' signals; as far as
modellers are concerned American block signals
which authorise stop and proceed moves have
pointed arms and all others are square or rounded. There are though many variations.

Most passenger railways in the world use the
block system in which the line is divided into
sections. At the boundary of each section is
either a signalbox (usually where mechanical
signalling survives) or a block signal (semaphore
or colour-light), controlled electrically either re-
motely from a signalbox some miles away, or
automatically by the passage of trains ahead.
The block system is either absolute (one train
only in the section), or permissive (where a
second train is allowed to enter at caution into an
occupied section to proceed on sight). Additional
block signals are used to split up the distance
between stations or signal boxes to shorten
sections. For modelling purposes, if a train
occupies a block section, the starting or exit signal (or North American block signal) behind it
will display a danger (stop)indication to a following train. Permissive working in model form is
not really practical for the average layout and it
is a case of not more than one train in a section
on one line at one time.

In Britain and Europe there is normally no
specific difference in appearance between block
and station signals, other than the French type
carré and semaphore, where the only difference
is in meaning.

Fig 120 CPR RDC-2 Budd stainless steel railcar and gantry
with 'absolute stop' searchlight signals. (If positioned
diagonally they would correspond to 119B instead of 119A.)
W. A. Corkill

In modelling practice a section of track often has its electrical power supply interrupted by contacts (such as SB-1) to prevent over-running (see fig 122). If the signal is at danger the train will stop automatically. On large club layouts much ingenuity and knowledge of electronic or solid state circuitry is devoted to the problems of how to detect the presence of trains in a block section, and how to make them slow down and stop realistically and at the right place. Plug-in modules are commercially available for those lacking the necessary expertise to design their own equipment (fig 129). Photo-electric cells can be positioned to view tracks diagonally so that any vehicle on the line will permanently activate a detection circuit (or to ring alarm bells if burglars visit the layout!). Semaphore signal control may be mechanical by levers and wires (fig 121) or by switch and solenoid (fig 122). The latter arrangement gives far more flexibility of control, with auxiliary contacts on the solenoid or on an interposing relay for numerous useful purposes.

Signal lamps can be lit by small grain of wheat bulbs, by light emitting diodes (LEDs) or by fibre optics, in which a central light source transmits light through thin plastic optical fibres to signals, station and yard lamps etc. Fibre ends are scraped and melted to form bulbs which glow with light and can be dyed in various colours. Thus even N and Z scale signals can have colour

to 'on' (ie 'caution') and light a red lamp on the control panel instead of a green one.

Terminal blocks TB interconnected by cables (of any length) enable wires to be checked, located or changed quickly and easily.

Colour-light signals can be operated by simple 2- or 3-position switches connected to lamp bulbs; but solenoids and relays must intervene if other tasks are to be performed.

Once these principles are understood, there is no limit to the complexity of signal control system which may be derived!

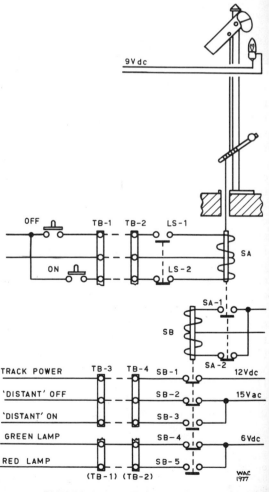

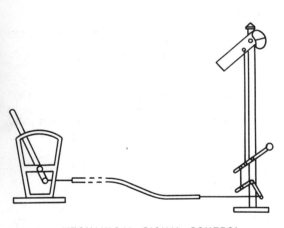

MECHANICAL SIGNAL CONTROL

Fig 121 Remote signals are operated by piano wire guided in metal tubing; sharp changes in direction are made by means of bell-crank levers, as shown.

Fig 122 Remote control is achieved electrically by means of pushbuttons on a control panel. As shown, the 'off' button has been pushed, causing solenoid SA to pull the signal 'off' (ie to the 'proceed' position, as shown). At the same time, auxiliary contact SA-2 has closed, activating interposing relay SB; *and* limit switch LS-1 has opened to prevent burning out SA by holding the pushbutton down too long; and LS-2 has closed ready for operation of the 'on' button. Contacts of SB have re-connected power to the track (SB-1); pulled 'off' the distant signal (SB-2) and lit a green lamp on the control panel.

When the 'on' button is pushed, SA returns the signal to the 'stop' position; LS-2 opens and LS-1 closes; and contacts of SB cut off power to the track (automatically stopping trains attempting to pass the signal), return the distant signal

ELECTRICAL CONTROL OF SEMAPHORE SIGNAL

lights of scale size! Slow operation of signals (and level crossing gates or barriers) can be obtained by passing a current through Nichrome wire, which expands slowly and allows a spring to move the signal arm.

Signals and accessories (for example level crossing barriers or gates) can be activated by the passage of trains. A most popular conventional device nowadays is the reed switch consisting of a thin magnetically operated contact enclosed in a small glass or plastic sealed tube or flat container laid between the rails. Small magnets mounted beneath locomotives or vehicles cause the contacts to close momentarily, thus completing the circuit to activate a relay. Relays are a subject in themselves; they may be continuously or momentarily rated, high or low resistance, simple or latching. And they all have their own little idiosyncrasies which make it unwise to delve too deeply without expert guidance. High frequency circuits can be used to transmit several signals simultaneously over the same wires or track. An obvious use is for constant brilliance

Prototype signals:
Fig 123 GWR lower quadrant. **124** BR colour-light with route indicator above. **125** SNCF *carré rouge*. *W. A. Corkill*
Fig 126 North American upper quadrant. *CPR.*

train lighting, with which a high frequency current lights the lamps but is prevented by suitable filter circuits from affecting the driving motor or motors. (Similar effects may be achieved with

Fig 127 German HO scale signals: Märklin semaphore with operating solenoid attached *(left);* Conrad ten-light colour-light starting, distant and shunting signal *(right)*. Short signs are *(left to right)* gradient post, A-*anfang* (start) and E-*ends* (finish) of speed restriction, H-*halte!* (stop here), W-*warte!* (wait here).

Fig 128 'Signalman Moore' at Selhurst controls.

circuits which pass a constant current at all voltages above a certain value which is too low to cause driving motors to work; thus a locomotive can stand still with its headlight or lights fully lit.) Another use is to control several locomotives on the same track section individually by means of coded 'pulse power' which is received selectively by filter circuits in locomotives.

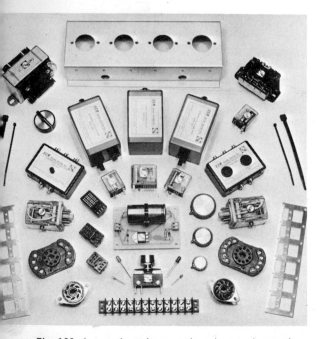

Fig 129 Automatic train controls, relays and capacitor-discharge turnout-control unit by ECM.
ECM

Fig 130 The Night Mail To Berlin; all lit up, making 'smoke' and ready to go.
Märklin

CHAPTER TEN
LOCOMOTIVES AND ROLLING STOCK

Locomotives and rolling stock are often chosen for emotional or sentimental reasons, regardless of their unsuitability for operating on a small or embryonic layout. Here is a conflict of interests which must be resolved if the layout is not to become a mere depository for large and colourful express passenger engines!

Beginners need one or two of the simplest and most reliable motive power units for testing newly-laid track and for pulling short trains from A to B; the *Flying Scotsman* or Big Boy can wait. The additional complications of many wheels and external moving parts of a large steam type locomotive on a small layout present some hazards; modern diesel locomotives with bogies that can usually negotiate undulating track are often found to have the fewest external moving parts and the most reliable operating characteristics.

Reliable as modern proprietary models usually are, they can all suffer from electrical troubles due to dirty wheels, bent pick-up wires or motors clogged with oil or dirt. Delicate valve gear and coupling rods on steam types can be easily bent by mishandling, causing stiff or erratic running. That is why at least one standby unit should always be maintained in good running order, ready for the unexpected arrival of visitors. At exhibitions, crowds stir up clouds of tiny dust particles which settle on the track and on all oily surfaces, gently increasing the need for standby power.

Compatibility is an important consideration, for it is little use having a train of attractive vehicles if they cannot be coupled together, or to a locomotive. Ideally, all locomotives and vehicles on a layout should have identical couplings; but this may restrict the choice to a small number of makes or may cause crippling cost if the standard type selected has to be separately purchased and fitted to many vehicles. The answer is to marshall vehicles having non-standard couplings into permanently-coupled short trains, each of which has a standard coupling at each end. Thus a standard equipped locomotive can couple up and pull or shunt, not individual vehicles, but at least groups of them. The SR electric trains at East Croydon and the transcontinental Dominion set at Whiskeyjack run permanently coupled, but local goods and passenger trains which are constantly being re-marshalled have standard couplings throughout.

With locomotives, compatibility also means the ability to couple together and work smoothly in twos or threes at all speeds and with all loads. At Folkestone Harbour the Continental Expresses and the empty Golden Arrow Pullman car train were hauled uphill by as many as four 0-6-0Ts, both ex-SECR and ex-GWR types being

Fig 131 Hornby 76(OO)16.5 BR class 55 Deltic diesel (the world's most powerful single-unit type when built in 1961) passes a Freightliner train in the rockery.

Fig 132 LMS 76(OO)16.5 Beyer-Garratt 2-6-0+0-6-2 No 47999 with two motors.
Millholme Models

used. To model such a scene we require a group of identical mechanisms (motors, gears and wheels) on which to fit identical or, if we please, different locomotive bodies. Taking the idea to the extreme, it is possible to make a reasonably good model of an LMS Beyer-Garratt 2-6-2+ 2-6-2 using two 0-6-0T mechanisms, but the Garratt is unlikely to need much assistance from an 0-6-0T!

Another point to watch is the tendency of very long locomotives or vehicles to push shorter ones sideways off the track on sharp curves, or very heavy vehicles to mow down lighter ones when going downhill or stopping quickly. For this reason the heaviest freight cars are always marshalled at the front of 50-car trains passing Whiskeyjack; the damage they could do if situated at the rear does not bear thinking about!

Model locomotives may outwardly resemble reciprocating steam, steam turbine, gas turbine, diesel (including diesel-electric or diesel-hydraulic) or electric prototypes. Inwardly, they are usually driven by clockwork, live steam or electric motor, the latter being almost universal nowadays. Reciprocating steam prototypes were in widespread general use from about 1840 to 1950, after which diesel and electric traction took over at an increasing rate. Precise times vary from country to country, but significant milestones were electrification of the Simplon tunnel in 1906 and operation of the CNR International Ltd in 1928 using two huge British-engined diesel locomotives.

Experimental locomotives of great technical interest included Swedish, PRR and LMS steam turbine-driven types, several gas turbine types, such as the powerful GE units operating at high altitudes on the UP in the 1950s, and ultra-high steam pressure machines of which the enormous CPR T-4-a class 3-cylinder 2-10-4 was perhaps the most successful. In 1931–4, this unique monster was in heavy freight service on the Mountain Subdivision. Such machines as these deserve to be modelled more often.

Electric prototypes differ little externally, except for older types having external rod drives and modern ones having several pantographs enabling them to receive current from overhead wires at different voltages. This is necessary for through running between, say, 25kV ac routes in France, 15kV ac routes in the German-speaking countries and 3kV dc routes elsewhere. Selection of correct prototype or model electric locomotives could lead us into technicalities far beyond the scope of this chapter, but one other type deserves mention. It collects current from a third rail alongside or between the running rails.

Rod-drive diesels for shunting duties are quite common but mainline or road types have transmissions hidden between the wheels. They have two main types of superstructure, developed from early GM productions, the cab unit and the hood unit (53). The former is just a box on wheels, while the latter has external platforms and handrails alongside the engine compartment.

Clockwork mechanisms use a spring driving the wheels through spur gears under control of a simple mechanical governor. They are wound up by means of a key; stopped, started or reversed by projecting levers; or controlled automatically by ramps and keys projecting from between the rails to engage with levers between the driving wheels. They were popular up to about 1938, after which development of small, reliable electric motors and introduction of popular table-top scales began to render them obsolete. The only obvious use for them today is on garden tracks negotiating long and inaccessible tunnels where electrical pick-up from the rails could be a serious problem; battery-driven locomotives serve equally well. Live steam, mentioned in Chapter One, deserves its own separate literature.

Electric motor drives are divided into alternating and direct current types; with 3, 5 or 7 poles and with speed reduction by spur gears or by worm and pinion. AC types have electromagnets for providing the field magnetism, and to reverse the direction of the armature or rotor (which rotates) it is necessary to switch over the electromagnet connections by means of a relay and latching mechanism which often take up as much space as a complete dc drive of equivalent power. DC types have permanent magnets and require no relays. The armature direction is reversed simply by reversing polarity of the track supplies (which are fed via wheels and/or frames to the motor brushes). The great majority of mechanisms today are for 12 volts dc.

Armatures with only three poles are difficult to run at very low speeds, unless aided by external flywheels (fig 135H) or pulse power. Four and six poles are not used due to a tendency for magnetic locking but five or seven poles give greatly improved slow-running characteristics.

Spur gearing is unable to give single-stage speed reduction of the required ratios (about 25:1 to 40:1) in the available space, so several stages are used, each using gears which have some flywheel effect. The mechanical advantage of each stage is low enough to permit rotation of the wheels by hand, which causes rotation of the armature 25 to 40 times faster. (This is *not* good practice.)

Worm drives achieve the entire speed reduction (and hence the entire mechanical advantage) in a single stage, but when the motor loses electrical power the mechanism locks up at once (unless fitted with external flywheel on an extension to the armature shaft). Better quality models normally use five-pole or seven-pole motors with worm drive, and with a sufficient number of electrical pick-up points to overcome jerky operation at discontinuities in the rails.

Electrical pick-up is assisted by using the maximum possible number of wheels (or skids, or pantographs). Normally, all driving wheels on one side of a locomotive are connected

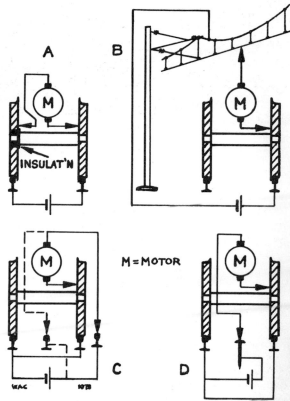

Fig 133 Locomotive current collection: A-two rail. B-overhead (with either two- or three-rail systems). C-three rail (alternative position shown dotted). D-stud contact.

directly to one of the motor brushes via a metal chassis; wheels on the *other* side are insulated by plastic inserts at the driving wheel hub or between the wheel proper and the outside, flanged tyre. These insulated wheels may pass current through pick-up wires (or even brake hangers) to the other motor brush, or their part may be taken over by tender wheels on the same side of the locomotive (figs 135A and G, 137).

Fig 134 Rivarossi/AHM N&W 87(HO)16.5 Y-6-b Mallet compound 2-8-8-2 with NEM type wheels and one cab-mounted motor driving both sets of wheels through pendular transmission.
Rivarossi photo

Fig 135 A is the *Rocket* with motor under the boiler; a larger motor would fit inside coach B. Or a motorised tender C propels a locomotive. Tank locomotive D has room for a large motor. Small tank engine E is helped by flywheel H. Mechanisms with spur gearing F are smoother at slow speeds; capacitor I across motor terminals reduces television interference. G has tender-mounted motor driving the wheels via a sliding 'dog clutch' compensating for movements between locomotive and tender.

Note: Two-rail current collection in E & F must be through driven wheels on either side of the frames but in other cases wheels shown black can be used as extra pick-up points.

Fig 136 *(below)* Locomotive A is electrically connected to auto-coach B. If the rails are fed with polarities shown and the train moves to the right it will conform with NEM602.

Fig 137 *(bottom)* 2-10-4 locomotive (fig 75) has a high-efficiency can motor A (whose armature rotates *outside* the central magnet). Gearbox B floats with sprung driving wheels and flexible drive C protects the motor from shocks and end thrusts. Limit switch D, driven by an axle-mounted square cam, enables sound unit E and loudspeaker F to produce synchronised exhaust sounds. Battery G and Switch H complete the unit Headlight I has a 'grain-of-wheat' bulb.

Fig 138 The Orient Express approaches Aix-Les-Bonnes-Jouef SNCF 87(HO)16.5 compound 4-8-2 No 241P7 has a motorised tender; so has Hornby LMS 5P5F 4-6-0 No 5154 *Lanarkshire Yeomanry* in fig 87.

On cheaper steam outline models the driving wheels are carried on axles passing through holes drilled in the chassis frames, no flexibility being provided. More expensive models, especially large North American types made in Japan or Korea, have driving wheels (all flanged) carried in brass axle boxes supported from the frames by coil springs. The Selkirk model in fig 75 has spring suspension on *all* wheels on locomotive and tender, giving a smooth ride and continuous electrical pick-up through eight locomotive and six tender wheels. The multiple-unit F7 diesel locomotive (in 53) picks up or returns current through a total of 24 wheels, electrically inter-connected. What, though, can be done for the 0-4-0 shunter having, at most, two pick-up points each side? If it proves too vulnerable to involuntary halts at rail discontinuities, it will help to couple it permanently to a four-, six- or preferably eight-wheel vehicle picking up current on all wheels and transmitting it to the locomotive through inconspicuous jumper wires which can resemble flexible brake pipe connections. The 0-4-4T can run permanently coupled to its auto-trailer coach (fig 136) for the same purpose. A simple single- or double-pole plug and socket made from brass rod and tube, or a screw connection, can be used to permit disconnection of the locomotive for maintenance.

Working pantographs on electric locomotives and railcars can provide a very smooth, reliable source of current if the wires are correctly installed and the pantograph springs maintain

a suitable tension. Pantograph-fitted (or third-rail) locomotives may be operated independently from others collecting current through the running rails. Such a locomotive picks up current from the overhead wire (or third rail) and returns it through one running rail. Steam or diesel locomotives use both rails for current collection. Thus, an electric-hauled train may be assisted up a steep hill by a steam or diesel locomotive at the rear, which slows down, stops and reverses on reaching the summit without affecting control of the train locomotive. Again, an electric shunting locomotive may operate on a section of track already occupied by a two-rail locomotive (as in a busy station or marshalling yard). Separate controllers are, of course, necessary and the electric locomotive must have its wheels insulated on one side of the chassis.

Motor mounting positions are fairly standard for most modern prototypes, but call for some ingenuity when dealing with Stephenson's *Rocket* or other ancient machines. The easiest solution is to mount the motor in a coach or wagon (fig 135B) and let *that* push the locomotive along; the next easiest is to motorise the tender, piling coal on top to hide any protruding parts (fig 135C). Triang, however, found it possible to fit a small motor and gears inside the *Rocket* locomotive itself, making a successful and popular novelty item on sale some years ago (fig 135A).

Some common motor mounting positions for rigid-suspension and flexible-suspension models are shown in figs 136/7. Where locomotives have spring-suspended driving wheels and the motor is rigidly mounted on the main frames, a flexible connection consisting of rubber, nylon tube or coiled steel wire is used (137C). Mechanical connections, are needed which allow for variation of distances between locomotive and tender on curves or with direction of motion.

Articulated locomotives having two separate mainframes and only one motor driving both sets of wheels pose a special problem, which may be solved by use of a pendular transmission as used in Rivarossi plastic-bodied models.

Locomotive construction gives untold pleasure but takes much time and a fair amount of skill. Beginners should therefore start with commercial ready-to-run locomotives and then if they feel like trying their hand go first for simple proprietary products and then assembly of white metal kits which fit over a proprietary chassis; this enables them to build up a stud of compatible locomotives. These kits may be assembled with glue or low melting-point solder; both methods should first be tried and mastered on inexpensive goods wagon kits. The next stage is to try a kit in which mainframes, wheels, axles, gears and motor have also to be assembled. Finally, if you want to go in at the deep end, you can start with a fresh sheet of drawing paper, a scale rule, some photographs of the prototype, some sheets of brass or nickel silver and a set of metalworking tools. Scratchbuilding is genuine craftsmanship, but constructors of a large layout can rarely find the time required. They may prefer to repair and modify existing models, acquiring any number of damaged or wrecked examples for the sake of a spare tender here, a chimney or a pair of wheels there.

Rolling stock can be modified or kit-bashed or even more frequently, especially the plastic-bodied types which are so easily cut, filed and glued with polystyrene cement. You want a coach 50ft long but can only buy a 60-foot model? Easy! You cut a section out of the 60ft model, join the parts together and fill in any little gaps with body putty, file and emery paper the sides smooth again, and repaint. Light, free-running plastic-bodied rolling stock with pin-point axles is very popular and very suitable for all layouts, but kits with sides stamped or engraved out of brass or nickel silver sheets have more detail and even greater realism (142). These require careful handling, very fine, clean files and often a knowledge of soldering for best results. Solder, brass etc. are much heavier than plastics, so one must take care not to overload the available motive power. It is wise to use plastics for long trains and heavy metal bodies for vehicles in short trains.

You will notice that we have not mentioned specific types or makes of locomotives and rolling stock. Such is the large variety now available, that you need only to look carefully through the various makers' lists and catalogues to find what you want.

Couplings may be working or non-working; ramp- or magnet-controlled; with or without advance operation. They may be made from plastics, metal die-castings or wire. Non-working couplings may be either the hook and chain European type or the North American Buckeye coupler. Either type involves manual intervention and the latter requires one vehicle to be lifted to couple up.

Working couplings fall into types where a moving component travels sideways to engage and those where movement is vertical. A ramp in the track, raised and lowered by hand, or electromagnet, forces the moving component out of its normal running position, in which it is held by gravity or by a light spring. All the principal makers have their own proprietary coupling systems, such as Märklin, Fleischmann, Triang/Hornby/Wrenn, or the widespread North American plastic hook-and-horn device, attributed to the NMRA. The latter works well for short trains but can sometimes be damaged by powerful locomotives. In N scale, standardisation is almost universal, using a well-designed and efficient vertical-lift type coupling.

Rivarossi use a magnetically operated vertical-lift type with an extra component which ensures that vehicles remain uncoupled after passing over a magnet set between the rails, *as long as a locomotive continues steadily pushing*. The locomotive may thus leave the vehicle anywhere at will and then withdraw. This useful facility is also available with the American Kadee type in which a projection resembling a disconnected brake hose is made to move by a track magnet; thus opening the jaws of the Buckeye coupler. When carefully adjusted and maintained, this is the finest of them all. It is readily available in O, HO and N scales.

Most types and makes of couplings are sold separately as spares, but the spares catalogue at a large model supplier (such as Beatties of London, La Maison des Trains in Paris or W. Schüler & Co in Stuttgart) may have to be consulted in some instances. Kadee and other North American types are usually available from importers, or from North American model shops.

CHAPTER ELEVEN
FINISHING TOUCHES

The most realistic layouts are not necessarily complicated, or even completed, but they have a workaday or 'lived in' appearance. Tracks are ballasted; rails are painted in a rusty, dusty shade of matt paint; telegraph poles, fences, mileposts, gradient and whistle posts appear in suitable places; tunnel-mouths are blackened with soot; walls are streaked with brown and green stains where drain water has trickled down; engine-sheds, goods sheds, factories and the like have spare parts, boxes, bits of timber, tools and piles of discarded junk lying about; and there are people going about their daily tasks.

People appear in many illustrations, carefully placed to lend credence to scenes. With a fisherman at the side of a canal lock, who would question the authenticity of the lock? And notice how track workers attract the eye and cause one to take the track itself for granted.

Likewise, a set of plausible looking passengers can stand on the plainest of station platforms and make the scene realistic.

Working accessories such as illuminated signal lamps or locomotive headlamps can aid realism, and sound effects can create a great deal of atmosphere. They can be tape recorded for general effect, with an occasional steam train running in time with the tape, or they can be generated by the train itself through a cam fitted to a driving axle and a locomotive-mounted sound unit and loudspeaker (137F). Locomotive whistles can be simulated by electronic devices, and smoke units fitted inside locomotive chimneys produce something resembling exhaust steam. Fibre optics enable lineside street lamps, neon signs etc to be modelled realistically in every scale.

Trackwork is finished by filling in gaps and

Fig 139 An Atlas 160(N)9 plastic-bodied ATSF stainless steel observation car. Standard 12-wheel 'heavyweight' cars appear in fig 70, and wooden 8-wheelers in figs 15 and 94.

Fig 140 A Hornby 76(OO)16.5 refrigerator van with under-frame linkage guiding the centre wheel-set on sharp curves. Other plastic-bodied wagons and vans appear in figs 16, 50 and 91.

Fig 141 From Copenhagen to Catania, elegant CIWL cars like this France-Trains 87(HO)16.5 plastic-bodied sleeping car graced Europe's finest trains.

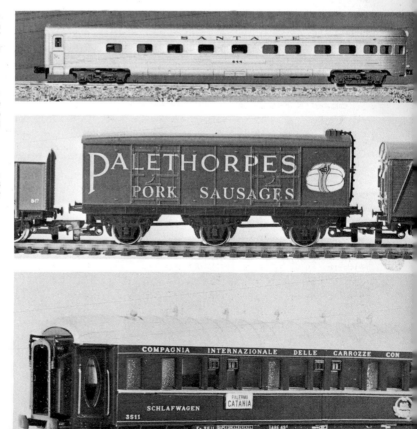

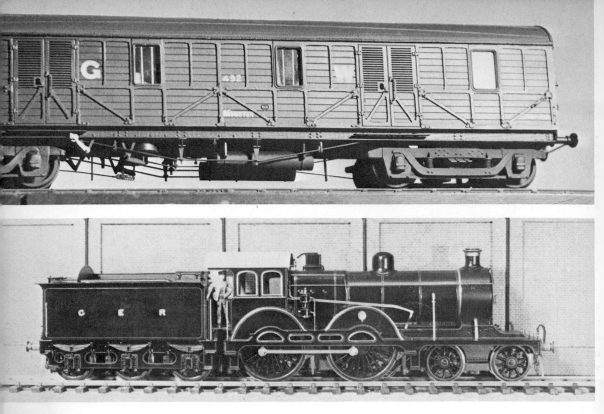

British brass kits: **142** *(above)* A Kemilway etched brass 76(OO)16.5 GWR 'Monster' van *Kemilway*. **143** *(below)* a shiny blue, professionally-painted kit-built Mallard 43.5 (O) 32 GER 4-4-0 by R. D. Baker.
J. Brown.

rounding off edges of the ballast with putty, mastic or modelling compound before brushing over with thin glue and dusting with fine ballast (stone chippings, sawdust etc), being careful to avoid fouling moving parts. Numerous methods are available for 'ballasting' which involve dropping water, glue and wetting compounds on to the line with eye droppers, or spraying them on with aerosols; all need to be tried out on a piece of test track before widespread use as results tend to vary considerably. A thin coat of light grey or brown matt paint completes the job. All running rails must be wiped absolutely clean but check rails are left in a rusty condition.

Rolling stock is hardly ever seen in immaculate condition, and a few miles of travel will suffice to raise dust covering wheels and axleboxes at least. Freight trains are never cleaned and these show numerous streaks and dribbles, colours depending on the type of traffic carried. Locomotives also collect dust on their wheels, as well as whitish or yellowish streaks where lime for water softening has been deposited by water or steam leaks or where a mixture of oil and steam has escaped from valves, flanges or cylinder glands. Steam escaping from safety valves on top of the boiler often contains lime which settles on the cab roof and tender top. Streaks of rust are common around the tender water filler, and also around the smokeboxes of locomotives worked so hard that the paint or graphite coating has been burnt off. For an example of a well used, or 'weathered' locomotive one could hardly improve on the Chinook Lumber Co Shay type, No 2 (144). This is a first-class model in brass by United, one of the best Japanese makes. All its parts work, including the piston-rods, valve gear, eccentric cranks, horizontal drive shafts, clutches and gears. It is a masterpiece of modelling, but as one never saw a lumber company Shay in exhibition paint finish it had to be weathered with matt grey, brown, white, yellow and rust colours. No wonder it needs oiling!

Painting metal locomotives or rolling stock is quite an art, and much practice is required. The model body (removed from its working components) is first stripped of all dirt, grease, soldering resin and old paint using a good paint stripper, acetone or a detergent degreasing jelly such as Swarfega, depending on the need. It is well rinsed in hot water, dried and inspected for stubborn deposits of old paint which may have to be removed with the point of a knife or a small screwdriver.

Brass models often come sprayed with clear varnish which has been baked on; this is hard to remove and can be painted over without difficulty. If, however, any repairs have been made using a soldering iron there will be areas with burnt and damaged varnish which must be carefully smoothed with very fine emery paper and treated as for bare metal.

Bare metal surfaces require etching with a primer, a thin coat of which is brushed or sprayed on, allowed to dry for 24 hours and then baked gently in a low heat such as the current of warm air from a convector heater for several hours. This helps to produce a really tough coat which resists scratching and chipping. A thin coat of matt undercoat paint is applied and baked as above, after which the surface is inspected in a strong light and rubbed smooth where necessary with a very fine emery paper or cloth. A second undercoat may be needed, after which the final gloss or semi-matt coat is applied. After baking, this is inspected for flaws, touched up and smoothed off where necessary, and baked again.

Water slide transfers, *decalcomane* (or decals in North America) are applied by soaking in water or recommended solvent and gently sliding on to the paint surface. They are available in a very wide range of railway company lining and lettering schemes and they all adhere best to a glossy or semi-matt surface (*not* a matt one).

Fig 144 Chinook Lumber's No 2 is a United brass 87 (HO) 16.5 Shay geared locomotive 'weathered' by the author. The 200-ton crane *(behind)* is railroad company property.

Special solvents such as Solvaset are brushed over them once in position and freed from bubbles of air; these soften the film and make them snuggle down over rivets and other projections. In this condition they are very delicate and care is needed to position them correctly or to readjust quickly after applying solvent. Dry print may be rubbed on instead of using transfers, but once on it cannot be moved about and a mistake means rubbing off and starting again. Gold leaf is similar and can be used for patching up dry print gold lining, or on its own.

Varnishing protects the paint and seals in the transfers or dry print. It can be glossy or matt or any mixture in between. It must be applied gently and sparingly at first, or lining may dissolve or distort. Spraying paint or varnish takes practice and needs care. Be particularly careful with aerosols for they can be harmful to health in certain circumstances. Follow manufacturers' instructions and if you must use them, do so in *well ventilated* conditions, avoid fumes and do not smoke while spraying. Brushing with plenty of well thinned paint on a good brush can often produce equally good results, but quick, confident application is essential.

CHAPTER TWELVE

OPERATION AND MAINTENANCE

Operating possibilities have been considered in Chapter Three, and trains of various types have appeared in illustrations but now it is time to summarise and to see what is involved in operating a layout.

Passenger trains include single or multiple railcars, push-pull or auto trailer locomotive-hauled units; stopping, suburban or commuter trains; semi-fast or fast express trains. They usually have accommodation for passengers' baggage in a brake-third or full brake (luggage van). They may have a dining car or a Pullman parlour car, or sleeping cars at night. Mail vans or travelling post offices may be attached. On Continental boat trains they may have first, second and third class accommodation, depending on the period. European international express passenger trains have vehicles of many nationalities, or might include International Sleeping Car Company (Wagons Lits) sleepers or diners, or be formed entirely of red and cream Trans Europe Express stock. North American transcontinental services are, or were, a vital link with remote settlements and therefore carried far more than just passengers. A typical train is the Dominion (CPR No 7, Montreal to Vancouver) as seen at Whiskeyjack. It has an express refrigerator car, or reefer; a rail postal car, or travelling post office; a baggage and express (ie express parcels) car; a day coach or chair car; four sleeping cars; dining car; five more sleeping cars; observation-parlour car. Total 15 cars.

Parcels and van (in North America, express) trains carry parcels, mail, milk churns, urgent perishables, horseboxes, etc, making short but interesting loads for passenger locomotives in between other duties. They are very likely to pick up and set down vehicles at stations along the line, although this is not quite so common with passenger trains. The latter sometimes split up to serve different destinations such as seaside resorts in Devon and Cornwall, and engine-changing was at one time a popular activity at large junctions. In North America, however, locomotive runs increased from about 1930 until a 1,000 mile run was commonplace. CPR and CNR diesels regularly run from

Montreal to Vancouver and back without change (a 5,800-mile round trip). Freight trains vary from slow pick-up goods (way-freights or peddlers) which serve every station yard and siding on their route, to fast scheduled services (hotshots or time freights) running nearly at passenger train speeds. Block trains carry a single commodity, such as coal, oil, motor vehicles, iron ore or containers, and there is little operating potential with them. They can be found today on most systems.

Service trains (work extras) include loads of rails, sleepers, or ballast; snowploughs or breakdown cranes (wreckers). There are also service vehicles providing for stores, tools, workshops, canteens and sleeping accommodation for railway workers.

Interesting operations centre around stopping passenger and pick-up goods trains; all others tend to run continuously from one end of the layout to the other without doing much on the way. Stopping passenger services call at every station, pick up and set down extra coaches and vans, change engines, terminate at some intermediate station and return to starting point. Pick-up goods trains may do all this as they go from siding to siding, and in addition they may 'shunt the yard', moving all vehicles around before departing. They may deliver logs to a sawmill and collect sawn lumber, or exchange full for empty coal wagons, or move empty cattle trucks alongside the stock pens ready for loading. That is what they do; how they do it is a matter of operating procedure.

Timetables can be drawn up for all trains and light engine movements during a period of, say, one hour; these tell operators stationed at control panels what trains to expect, and when. Often a scale clock is used, covering perhaps ten scale hours in one hour. Thus a run of half a minute between stations takes five scale minutes as per timetable. A designated locomotive moves off shed to pick up a rake of coaches and backs them into the terminus to await starting time. When that time comes, signals and turnouts are set for the train to reach its first stop, where it arrives (we hope) on time.

Signalmen 'offer' the train to their colleagues

at the next control panel, who 'accept' it and set their part of the route for it. Then, at scheduled departure time, it moves on. At its destination, the locomotive is uncoupled, a station pilot removes the coaches, and the light engine retires on shed for servicing and turning ready for its return working.

Freight train working is more complicated in that each individual vehicle is designated by its number (eg LNER coal wagon No 999999), its pick-up point and its destination. Operators must use their own ingenuity and skill to move cattle truck No 555444 from the far end of a siding at Shuntingdon to the middle of a rake of assorted vehicles deposited alongside the stock pens at Umbergate without, of course, obstructing the passage of numerous express passenger and fast freight trains scheduled to use the same line during the move.

Some vehicles or trains are restricted to certain tracks on account of their weight or dimensions; all signals must be correctly identified and obeyed, and speed restrictions must be observed where they are in force. North American operators also follow the rulebooks in sending out flagmen (simulated with coloured pins) to protect the rear of trains stopped on the right of way and in giving all the appropriate whistle signals (of which the morse letter Q (– – – –) for a level crossing is the best known).

Maintenance prevents unnecessary interruptions to train services and involves regular attention to track, turnouts, locomotives and rolling stock. Once every six months at least, operations should be suspended until all equipment has been serviced on the following lines. Running rails are cleaned with a moderately strong degreasing fluid such as acetone or carbon tetrachloride (which must be used with care in a well ventilated room—and nobody should smoke —as fumes can be harmful) and rubbed over with a dry cloth. Plastic materials must not come in contact with cleaning fluid as they can be damaged. In damp climates a light smear with lubricating oil helps to retard oxidation. Hard deposits of oxide, carbon dust and oil can be dislodged by prodding with a sharp screwdriver or chisel, being careful not to damage the rail surface. Badly pitted areas are smoothed with fine emery cloth and most dull metal surfaces can be brightened with abrasive blocks or erasers sold by model shops. After cleaning comes removal of dust and debris with a dry paintbrush or small vacuum cleaner, and checking for bends, kinks

and twists. Moving parts of turnouts are carefully examined and adjusted if necessary.

Locomotive wheels collect a mixture of oil and dust which forms a hard ring, causing unsteady running and sparking. A wipe over with a rag dipped in acetone may help but often the ring has to be eased off with the tip of a sharp penknife, taking *great* care not to scratch the nickel or chrome plating of wheel tyres and flanges. In bad cases it is advisable to remove the motor or gearbox so that driving wheels can be turned easily. Sandpaper or emery cloth should not be used but soft balsa wood helps with polishing and with removal of light deposits of dirt. Coach and wagon wheels should be dealt with similarly. Ideally all track, locomotives, and rolling stock should be cleaned in one operation. It is useless to do part only since dirt from uncleaned parts will quickly be spread by wheels back to the cleaned parts.

All surfaces through which electricity passes to the motor brushes, including tender wheels, tender bogie (truck) frames and bearings, and the connections between locomotive and tender must be clean and bright, while contact between all components in electrical circuits must be positive and firm. Weak springs and frayed wires are replaced.

Motors are cleaned by removing brushes and rotating the commutator against a dry cloth or piece of balsa wood until clean and bright. Acetone may be used sparingly if necessary but the surface must on no account be scratched with sandpaper or sharp tools. Slots between commutator segments collect carbon dust which is removed carefully with the point of a needle. Brushes are rubbed smooth with very fine emery cloth wound round a pencil or a metal rod of suitable diameter; if badly worn or pitted they should be replaced.

Frames and bearings are wiped clean of grease and dirt and all working parts are lubricated with one or two tiny drops of special acid-free oil from instrument makers or model shops. Nylon gears need synthetic lubricants from specialist firms like LaBelle and suppliers of plastic framed models usually advise the correct type of oil or grease to use. Commutators and brushes of electric motors are *never* oiled or greased; only the bearings at each end of the armature shaft, and then sparingly.

Couplings of every locomotive and vehicle should be cleaned and adjusted if necessary; couplings may well be too high, too low or, very possibly, bent to one side.

Ammeters and voltmeters help diagnose faults, but locomotive headlights (or a test lamp connected across the rails) can give useful information. Full volts at the control panel but no amps (and no light) indicates an open circuit or loose connection; low volts and a high current (and a dim light) indicates a short circuit. A bright light in conjunction with a stationary locomotive indicates either an open circuit such as sticking motor brushes or a partial short circuit through a stalled armature which is mechanically locked, often by bent valve gear

or a piece of wire jammed between the wheels. The latter condition is dangerous as it causes overheating of the windings and demagnetisation of the permanent magnet in dc motors. Demagnetised motors draw heavy currents, overheat, and develop little or no power. Faults and gremlins are many and mysterious, but careful maintenance eliminates most of them and ensures many hours of happy operating.

Fig 145 Journey's End: the last passenger has gone, and Bridgewater station pilot No **6530** is about to remove the empty coaches.
J. Brown

APPENDIX ONE

GRAPHICAL METHODS FOR SCALING

The diagram (fig 146) shows graphically the relationships between prototype dimensions and model dimensions in a range of popular scales.

To convert 40mm in OO scale, or 40mm/1ft, to the corresponding figure for gauge O, or 7mm/1ft, we project a line horizontally from 40mm on the vertical or model axis to intersect the 4mm/1ft line; from there we project vertically up to interesect the 7mm/1ft line, project horizontally from the point of intersection back to the vertical axis and read off the answer; 70mm. In this example the figures chosen were easy to compute in one's head, but odd amounts require the use of a desk calculator, slide rule or graphs. Similarly 145mm in 10mm/1ft scale corres-

ponds to 20.3mm in 1.4mm/1ft scale; or to 14.5ft on the prototype. The larger the scale to which a graph is drawn, the greater the accuracy with which it may be used.

Suppose we wish to adopt some entirely new scale of, say, 5.3mm/1ft; we can do this by erecting vertical lines from the 10, 20 and 30ft points on the horizontal axis and noting where they intersect horizontal lines drawn from (5.3×10), (5.3×20) and (5.3×30) ie 53, 106 and 159mm on the vertical axis. A straight line drawn through the three points of intersection will be the desired conversion line for 5.3mm/1ft scale. And so on.

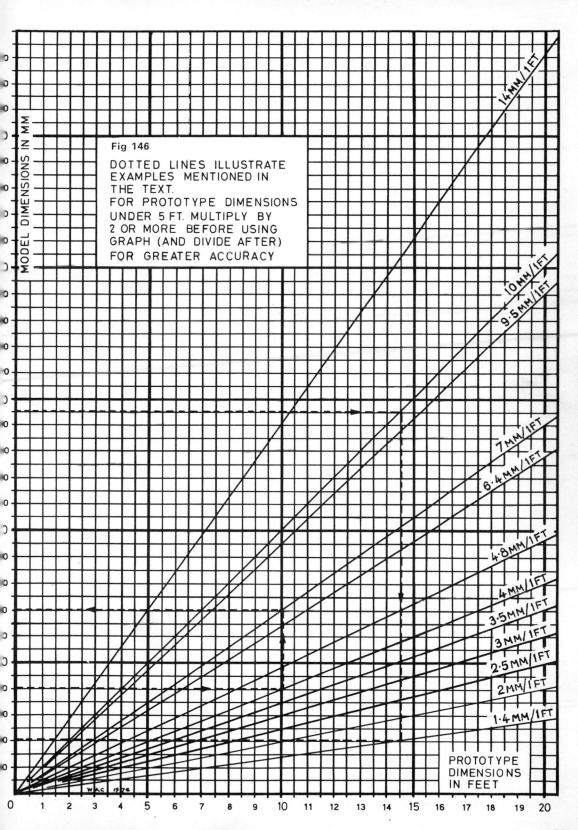

MODEL DIMENSIONS IN MM

Fig 146

DOTTED LINES ILLUSTRATE
EXAMPLES MENTIONED IN
THE TEXT.
FOR PROTOTYPE DIMENSIONS
UNDER 5 FT. MULTIPLY BY
2 OR MORE BEFORE USING
GRAPH (AND DIVIDE AFTER)
FOR GREATER ACCURACY

14MM/1FT
10MM/1FT
9·5MM/1FT
7MM/1FT
6·4MM/1FT
4·8MM/1FT
4MM/1FT
3·5MM/1FT
3MM/1FT
2·5MM/1FT
2MM/1FT
1·4MM/1FT

PROTOTYPE
DIMENSIONS
IN FEET

W.A.C. 1976

0 1 2 3 4 5 6 7 8 9 10 11 12 13 14 15 16 17 18 19 20

89

ELECTRICAL SUPPLIES AND CONTROLS

This appendix contains drawings, diagrams and descriptions illustrating the basic problems of power supply and locomotive control in two-rail dc systems. Some knowledge of electricity is required for full understanding of these problems and of the equipment employed for the solutions shown.

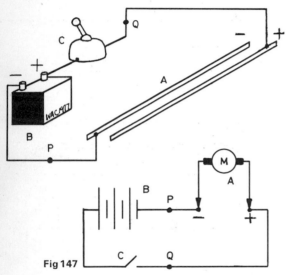

Fig 147

A primitive situation is shown in fig 147 where locomotive A rests on track connected by wires to the terminals of battery B, one of them containing on-off switch C. To change the direction of motion, the wires must be reconnected to the opposite terminals of the battery; but there is no means of altering the speed. The electrical diagram alongside the sketch shows the corresponding symbols which we shall use for ease of understanding. Terminals P and Q are used so that the battery and switch can be replaced by some other source of power any time we want. The locomotive is represented by its dc driving moter M (armature and brushes).

Controlled direct current from battery B is provided in fig 148 with the addition of rheostat (variable resistance) D and double-pole change-over switch E. The rheostat provides control of speed by varying the resistance in series with the motor, while the double-pole switch

reverses the voltage applied to the motor and hence changes its direction of rotation.

Rectified current is supplied in fig 149 by means of a transformer whose primary winding A is fed with 240 volts alternating current, single-phase. Note that there are two tappings to choose from; a 240V feed connected to the 110V tapping would produce excessive voltage and power in the secondary side, while a 110V feed connected to the 240V tapping would not produce enough. The transformer core B provides a magnetic flux path between the primary and secondary coils C and the latter is shown with a centre tapping. The outer ends of the coil are connected to rectifiers D in such a way that no matter which way the current flows one of the rectifiers is always conducting. Rectifiers, by definition, conduct in one direction only.

The current waveforms at A or C will resemble sine wave I, in which the *effective* voltage is the rms (root mean square) value, J. A 240V ac supply means 240V rms unless otherwise specified. The other important value is the peak value K which helps us to operate solenoids reliably. The waveforms of current passed simultaneously by the two rectifiers resemble L and M. Each

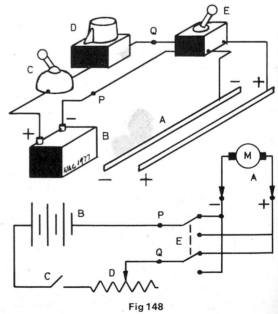

Fig 148

involves 'half-wave rectification' and if the output of *one* rectifier is reduced to zero the locomotive will react by producing its full torque (turning effort) but at a greatly reduced speed due to the reduced current and hence power available over a given time period.

By joining together the outputs of both rectifiers the wave form N is produced; this is 'full-wave rectification'. It is not as smooth as direct current from a battery, and to 'iron out the kinks' capacitor E is connected across the output wires, and choke (inductance) F is in series with one wire. These convert the waveform N to a steady dc with a small ripple, O.

Switch-fuse unit G enables the supply to be disconnected by hand or by the blowing of a fuse in the event of a short circuit. Instead of a fuse, a mechanical or thermal type circuit-breaker may be used; this may reset itself automatically after the fault has been cleared, or it may need resetting manually; many different types are available. A small indicator lamp is connected across the output wires to show when power is available.

Waveform PP shows 'pulse power', which differs from half-wave rectification; to increase train speed the *width* of the pulses increases, not the height. Thus the full torque is always available from the motor but for increasing periods of time. Modern transistorised controllers use pulse power, which is effective for starting sticky motors but generates noise and heat.

A competant arrangement such as can be achieved with variable transformer controllers in the medium price range is shown in fig 150. Controller A supplies 12V dc through two terminals; one is connected to a thick brass or copper busbar feeding a bank of on-off switches serving the nearside rails of five track sections, and the other is connected to the far side rail of each section. This arrangement is called common return wiring and it is much simpler than switching both wires to each section individually. Which rail is the feed and which the common return or neutral is immaterial provided they do not change places anywhere round the track; this could cause a short circuit.

Terminal strips C and D are connected by cabling (over any distance, short or long) which is insulated solid copper for dc and insulated stranded copper for ac. The heavier the copper section the better, and if one standard section of cable is used throughout, *two* wires are used for

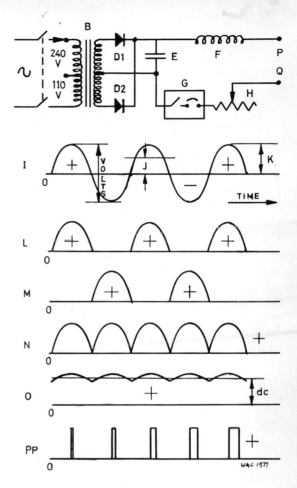

Fig 149

the longer runs, joined together at the ends. Terminal strips enable wires and cables to be identified and changed around, or extra circuits to be connected in, without spending hours tracing the ends of unknown cables in awkward positions beneath the baseboard. Colour coding can help, too (eg red for power feeds; black for common return; yellow for signal circuits etc).

Locomotives E and F stand on track sections 1 and 4 respectively. To operate them it is necessary to close switch No 1 or No 4; either can move without the other or, if required, they may both move but only in the same direction. To achieve this degree of choice, the track feed rails have been broken by inserting gaps with insulating rail joiners. Gaps always appear at the frog end of a turnout or a short distance beyond; rarely at the switch end because no engine could be parked there without interfering with all other

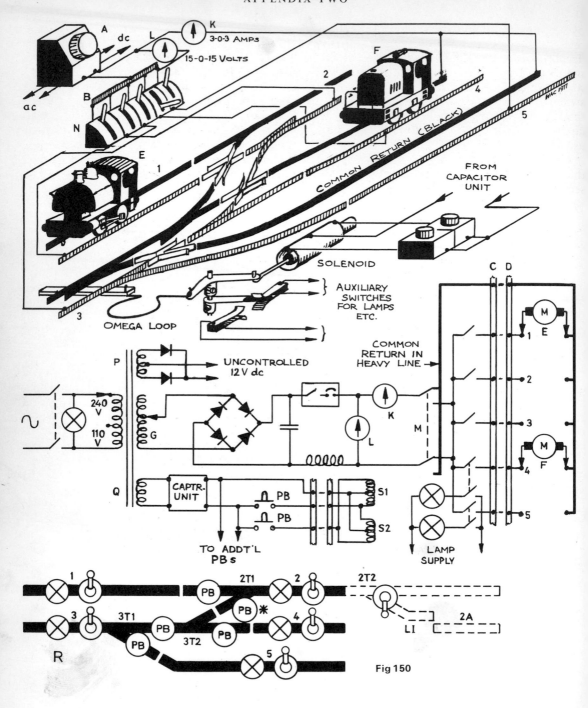

Fig 150

train movements over the turnout. Turnouts placed frog-to-frog need gaps in *both* rails to prevent short circuits—or dead frogs.

On the circuit diagram, G represents the variable transformer, with isolated auxiliary windings P and Q supplying uncontrolled dc and

ac for supplying (say) a rheostat feeding a narrow-gauge railway and a series of ac solenoids and relays for signalling etc.

Bridge rectifier H, capacitor I and inductance J provide smoothed full-wave dc; ammeter K measures current passing at a voltage measured by voltmeter L; and changeover switch M reverses the current when required. Switches N decide which section(s) of track shall be fed, and switch (eg No 5) has second poles connected in series with lamps and a battery. Thus when switch No 5 is closed a lamp lights to indicate that the track is live. This is how control panel lamps are activated. Locomotives are indicated, as before, by their driving motors.

Mimic diagram R on the control panel shows the operator where the track is sectioned, which sections are live or (by the direction of switch toggles as at 2T2) which way the turnouts are set. Turnouts may, of course, stick half way and in that case some more positive indication is required. The Hammant & Morgan SM3 double-acting solenoid is a typical commercial product for operating turnouts and signals which has auxiliary contacts changing over only when the moving parts are near the end of their travel; lamps connected in series with these contacts give a more reliable indication. LI is a removable link for isolation of track section 2A.

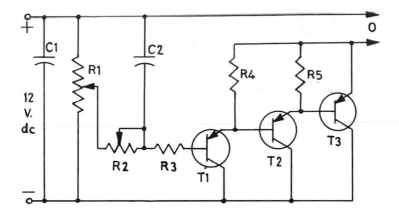

Fig 151 Transistor controller circuit: radio type potentiometer R1 is the speed control; it passes only a very small current but such is the amplification or 'gain' of a three-transistor unit that the power transistor T3 may feed *100 times* as much current to the track. T1 is the control transistor; T2 the amplifier transistor; the latter needs a small heat sink to prevent it overheating, while T3 needs a large one. Capacitor C2 and resistor R2 simulate the momentum of a real train by delaying the effects of any sudden alteration of R1. Other resistors and C1 smooth out surges and reduce leakages.

BIBLIOGRAPHY

There are hundreds of excellent books and periodicals dealing with every aspect of railways or railway modelling; it is impossible to list them all here. This bibliography covers only items for which precise or comprehensive information is difficult to locate. Not all items listed may be currently in print, but they will help to explain 'where it all came from'!

General:
Manuale del Fermodellista, R. Lobita, Briano Editore, Genova, 1963.
Modellbahn Handbuch, K. Gerlach, Albis Verlag, Düsseldorf, 1965.
World Railways, Sampson Low, Janes, London (annually).

Trackwork:
'Dimensions for Switches' (NMRA RP12 data) *Model Railroader,* July 1972.
'Permanent Way', P. W. Blythe, *Model Railway News,* October 1964.
'Printed Circuit Points', I. R. Blackbourne, *Railway Modeller,* June 1966.
'Protofour Policies', M. S. Cross, *Model Railroader,* August 1975.

Bridges:
'Bethlehem Twin-Span Turntable', *Model Railroader,* February 1973; December 1977.
Bridge & Trestle Handbook, P. Mallery, Simmons-Boardman, New York, 1958.

Signals:
British Railway Signalling, G. M. Kichenside & A. Williams, Ian Allan; London, 1963/78.
'French Signalling Practice', R. Stokes, *Railway World,* May, August, September 1969.
'From Policeman to Push Buttons' (European signalling), G. M. Kichenside, *Trains Seventy-one,* Ian Allan; London, 1970.
'La Signalisation', B. Renaudot, *Rail Miniature Flash,* September/October 1963.
Operating Rules, Book No 35609; Canadian National Rlys, Grand Trunk Rly System etc; Montreal, 1929.
'Signal Aspects And Indications', L. H. Westcott, *Model Railroader,* October 1970.

Electrical matters:
'Capacitor Discharge Power Supply' (for double-solenoid point motors, giving high power without risk of burnout), A. Ross, *Railway Modeller,* December 1974/November 1975.
'Doing It Digitally (Pt 11)', O. N. Bishop, *Everyday Electronics,* August 1977.
Electrical Handbook For Model Railroads, P. Mallery, vols 1 & 2, Carstens Publications, Fredon, NJ, 1974.
'Inertia Simulation At Low Cost', N. M. Narracott, *Railway Modeller,* May 1977.
'Model Train Control Methods—2', *Model Railroader,* February 1972.
'One Button-One Route' (Push Button Routing Systems), A. Ross, *Railway Modeller,* October/November 1964.
'Reeds and Relays (Automatic Control)', R. R. Waller, *Railway Modeller,* February 1974.
'Thyristor Control', M. Cole, *Railway Modeller,* July 1975.
'Trade Topics—(Can) Motors', *Model Railroader,* August 1972.
'Transistor Theory & Building The (Semi-Conductor Control) Unit', C. J. Freezer, *Railway Modeller,* August/September 1975.

Miscellaneous:
'A Coat of Paint' (deals with spray painting), C. J. Freezer, *Railway Modeller,* June 1975.
'Couplings (Hand-Built)', R. H. Middleton, *Model Railway Constructor,* July 1975.
'Live Steam In 1/240 Scale', A. A. Sherwood, *Model Railways,* November 1973.
'Midland Magnificence (Derby Museum Historical Layout)', D. A. Bell, *Railway Modeller,* October 1968.
Practical Geometry & Engineering Graphics, W. Abbott, Blackie, London, 1947.

ABBREVIATIONS

ac	alternating current
Am	American
ATSF	Atchison, Topeka & Santa Fé Railway
Br	British
BR	British Railways/British Rail
BRMSB	British Railway Modelling Standards Bureau
CIE	*Coras Iompair Eireann*/Irish State Railways
CIWL	*Compagnie Internationale Des Wagons-Lits Et Des Grands Express Euro-péens*/International Sleeping Car Company
CNR	Canadian National Railways
Cont	Continental European
CPR	Canadian Pacific Railway/CP Rail
DB	*Deutsche Bundesbahn*/German Federal Railway.
dc	direct current
DRGW	Denver & Rio Grande Western Railroad
EMD	Electro-Motive Division (of General Motors)
FS	*Ferrovie Dello Stato*/Italian State Railways
GCR	Great Central Railway (England) (Part of LNER from 1923)
GE	General Electric Company (USA)
GER	Great Eastern Railway (England) (Part of LNER from 1923)
GM	General Motors Corporation (USA & Canada)
GNR	Great Northern Railway (England) (Part of LNER from 1923)
GNR (I)	Great Northern Railway (Ireland)
GWR	Great Western Railway (England) (Now part of BR)
kV	kilovolt(s)
LBSCR	London, Brighton & South Coast Railway. (Part of SR from 1923)
LMS	London, Midland & Scottish Railway (1923-48) (Now part of BR)
LNER	London & North Eastern Railway (1923–48) (Now part of BR)
LNWR	London & North Western Railway (Part of LMS from 1923)
LT	London Transport (Railways)
MOROP	MOdelling in EuROPe standards organisation
MR	Midland Railway (England) (Part of LMS from 1923)
MSCR	Manchester Ship Canal Railway
N & W	Norfolk & Western Railroad (USA)
NA	North America
NCC	Northern Counties Committee (Ireland)
NEM	*Norme Europee Modellistiche;* standards issued by MOROP in the principal European languages.
NJ	New Jersey (USA)
NMRA	National Model Railroad Association (USA)
NP	Northern Pacific Railway (USA)
PRR	The Pennsylvania Railroad (Now part of Penn-Central)
SBB	*Schweizerische Bundesbahnen*/Swiss Federal Railways. Also known as *Chemins de Fer Féderaux/Ferrovie Federale Svizzere*
SECR	South Eastern & Chatham Railway (Part of SR from 1923)
SNCF	*Société Nationale Des Chemins De Fer Français*/French National Railways
SR	Southern Railway (England) (1923-48) (Now part of BR)
UP	Union Pacific Railroad
WP & Y	White Pass & Yukon Railway (Skagway, Alaska to Whitehorse, Yukon)

INDEX

Entries in italics indicate illustrations. Fig numbers are given in brackets.

abutments, *49 (71)*, 51 (73 H), 52-3, *(74 L & M), 53 (76)*
AC models, 45, *(see also* mechanisms)

backgrounds, *7 (6)*, 23 (24), 28, 29 *(35D)*, 36 *(53), 47 (70)*, 58-60, *60 (88-9), 63 (95), 67 (105), 75 (123)*
baseboards, 28-34, *29-34 (35-49)*
bridges: beam, 48, *49 (71J);* cantilever, *50 (72A),* 51; concrete, 48, *49 (71B);* masonry, *31 (41)*, 46 *(69)*, 48, *49 (71D & F)*, 55, 55-6 *(81-2), 57 (85), 59 (87);* movable, 46, *46 (69)*, 50, *50 (72B, C & D),* 56; plate girder, *31 (41)*, 36 *(53), 47 (70)*, 48-9, *49 (71E, K & L),* 51-3, *51-3 (73-5), 63 (94);* steel truss, *31 (41)*, 49, *49 (71M)*, 50 *(72)*, 53-4, *54 (78-80)*, 56 *(83-4);* suspension, 48, *49 (71A);* timber, *9 (9), 23 25E)*, 48, *49 (71Z)*, 50, 54, *54 (78C), 59 (87);* trestle, *9 (9), 23 (25E)*, 48, *49 (71V-Z), 59 (87) (see also* trestles)

catch points, *(see* derails)
catenaries, *(see* current coll, o/h)
clearances, 17, *17 (17)*, 20-3, *20 (22)*, 21 *(23)*, 23 *(25), 26 (33)*
code, scale/gauge, 14 (table 2), 15, 17, 17 (table 3)
common return wiring, 42, *43 (64c)*, 92 *(150)*
continental european modelling, 8, 11, *18 (20)*, 63 *(95-6), 67 (105)*, 71-3, *75 (125, 127)*, 76 *(130)*, 81 *(138)*, 83 *(141)*
controls, automatic, 74-5, *74 (122 SB-1)*, 76 *(129)*
controllers: half-wave effect, 45, 90-1, 91 *(149 L & M);* high-frequency, coded, 76; portable, 43; pulse power, 45, 91, 91 *(149 PP);* rheostat, 45, 90, *90 (148D)*, 91 *(149H);* transistor, 45, *93 (151);* variable transformer, 45, 90, 92 *(150 G) (see also* electrical)
control panels, 23 *(24)*, 29 *(35F, 36N), 43 (64)*, 44 *(65-8)*, 76 *(128)*
coupler, couplings, 17 *(18 E & F)*, 77, 82
current collection, electrical: overhead wire, 21, *31 (41)*, 42, *58 (86)*, 66-7, *67 (105-6)*, 72 *(118)*, 81; stud contact, 7, *25 (31)*, 42, *79 (133D);* three-rail, 41-2, *79* (133C); two-rail, *37 (54 I & N)*, 39 *(56)*, 40 *(57-8)*, 42, *42 (62-3), 43 (64), 79 (133A)*, 80 *(135-7)*, 81

derails, *19 (21)*, 41
DC models, 43, 45 *(see also* mechanisms)

electrical power supply, wiring, 35, 39, *39 (55-6)*, 42, *42 (62-3)*, 43, *43 (64)*, 44 *(65-7)*, 45, 90-3
expansion of track etc, 39, *39 (55)*, 48

faults, elec or mech, 35, *35 (51-2)*, 39, *42 (63)*, 77, 81, 87-8
fiddle yards, 26

garden railways, 5, 28, *34 (50)*, 77 *(131)*
gauges, loading, 14, 20
gauges, track, 12-17, *12 (12G)*, 12 (table 1), 14 (table 2), 17 (table 3)
gradients, profiles, 26-7 *26 (33)*

half-wave rectification, *(see* controllers)
historical modelling, *5 (2), 9 (9)*, 11, *80 (135A-C)*

industry, 23, *23 (25), 59 (87)*, 60, *63 (94), 75 (123)*
interlocking, 68, 74, *74 (122 SB-1)*
interlocking towers, *(see* signal boxes)

kits, kitbashing, *6 (4), 9 (9)*, 27 *(34)*, 31 *(41)*, 40 *(58)*, 54 *(80)*, 61, *61 (91)*, 82, *84 (142-3)*

layout plans: ambitious, *10 (10);* Brakewell, *70 (113);* Drachensee, *72 (117);* East Croydon, *26 (32);* Gigotville, *71 (115);* Llantaffy Wells, *24 (28);* Shuntingdon C, *25 (30);* Square C Quarry, *23 (25);* Tramworth, *26 (33);* wiring diagram, *43 (64)*
layouts, scenes: Aix-Les-Bonnes, SNCF, 8, *18 (20)*, *67 (105)*, 81 *(138)*, Bishop's Stratford, GER, *61 (91);* Bridgewater, LMS/LNER, *6 (3-5)*, 7, 66 *(103)*, 88 *(145);* Cache Lake, Skunk R, Whiskeyjack; CPR Mountain Subdivision; 7, 27, *27 (34)*, 36 *(53), 47 (70)*, 53 *(75), 63 (94)*, 77, 86; East Croydon, Selhurst, SR, 3, 7, *7 (6)*, 26, *60 (88)*, *64 (98)*, 76 *(128)*, 77; Gr Reunion Canal etc, BR, *31 (41);* Knoll's Grn, GWR, *25 (31);* McWheedle Mine, *59 (87);* Märklin, *10 (11);* Rabbit W Tunnel, BR, *58 (86), 67 (106);* Unterwald, DB, *24 (29)*, 85
lettering, lining, *6 (5), 61 (90), 63 (95), 83 (139-41)*, 85
L-girder baseboards, 31-3, *31 (43), 32 (44)*
Locomotives: articulated, 78, 78 (132), 79 (134), 82, *85 (144);* British, *3, 4 (1A), 5 (2), 6 (3 + 5)*, 13 *(14)*, 78 *(132)*, *84 (143)*, 88 *(145);* compatible, 77-8, *80 (136);* Cont Eur, *4 (1C)*, 24 *(29)*, 54 *(80)*, 67 *(105)*, 76 *(130)*, 81 *(138);* diesel, *16 (16)*, 36 *(53)*, 77 *(131)*, 78, *80 (135F);* electric, *31 (41)*, 58 *(86)*, 67 *(105 + 106)*, 78; industrial, *85 (144);* narrow-g, *15 (15)*, 24 *(29)*, *59 (87), 65 (101);* N American, *4 (1B)*, 13 *(14)*, 18 *(19)*, 27 *(34)*, 53 *(75)*, 79 *(134)*, 80 *(137)*, *85 (144) (see also* mechanisms)
loco facilities, *21 (23)*, 25 *(30)*, 27 *(34)*, 64-6, 64 *(97-8), 65 (100-1)*
lubrication, 87

maintenance, preventive, 87-8
masonry, 55, *55 (81)*, 56 *(82), 59 (87)*
mechanisms, clockwork or electrical, 78-9, *78(132), 79 (134), 80(135-7), 81(138)*
modern railway modelling, 11, *67 (105-6), 77 (131)*

Narrow-g modelling, 16-17, *19 (21), 23 (24-5)*, 24 *(29), 59 (87)*
N American modelling, 11, *18 (19)*, 27 *(34)*, 35-7, 36 *(53), 47 (70)*, 53 *(75), 63 (94)*, 73, *73 (119-20)*, *75 (126), 79 (134), 85 (144)*

operating, 22-6, 43, *44 (65-7)*, 76 *(128)*, 86-7

painting, 57-8, 84-5, *84 (143), 85 (144)*
plaster, of Paris, 57-8, *57 (85)*
points, *(see* turnouts)
portable baseboards, layouts, 28
power supplies, *(see* electrical)
push-pull trains, 24, *25 (31)*, 60 *(88)*, 80 *(136)*, 81

rack railways, 27, 41, *41 (61)*
railcars, *18 (20)*, 24, *73 (120)*

relays, 42, 74-5, *74 (122SB)*, 76 *(129)*, *(see also* solenoids)
return loops, *21 (23)*, 22, *23 (24-5)*, 42, *43 (64RL)*, 44 *(67)*
rheostats, resistors, *(see* contrlrs)
rocks, 57-8, *57 (85), 59 (87), 66 (104)*
rolling stock, *7 (6), 25 (31)*, 34 *(50), 47 (70)*, 54 *(79-80)*, 60 *(88-9), 63 (94)*, 77, 82, *83 (139-41)*, 84 *84 (142)*, 86-7
roundhouses, *(see* loco facilities)

scale models, 12, 13, *13 (13)*
scales: coarse/fine in g 'O', 16; converting, 19, 88 *89 (146);* popular, 5, 13-16, 14 (table 2), *15 (15), 16 (16)*, 17 (table 3);
signals, semaphore and colour-lt: block, 26, 73; British, *7 (6)*, 68-70, *68 (107), 69 (108-9)*, 70 *(110-13), 75 (123-4);* French, *67 (105)*, 71, 71 *(114-15), 75 (125);* German, 71-3, *72 (116-18), 75 (127*, Italian, 70, *70 (112);* N American, 73, *73 (119-20*, *75 (126);* 'train order', *18 (19), 47 (70), 73 (119C)* wiring (control), *74 (122)*
signal boxes, 66, *66 (102-3)*, 76 *(128)*, 77 *(131)*
slips *(see* turnouts)
solenoids, 42, *66 (104)*, 74, *74 (122SA), 75 (127)*
sound effects, *80 (137)*, 83
standards, 12, 35-7, *37 (54), 80 (136), (see also* gauges, scales)
standard components, 9, *10 (11)*, 19-23, *20 (22)*, 21 *(23)*
stations, *6 (4-5)*, 19 *(21)*, 24-6, 24 *(26-9)*, 25 *(30-1)*, 26 *(32-3), 47 (70)*, 60 *(88)*, 61-2, 61 *(90-1)*, 62 *(92-3), 63 (94-6)*, 72 *(118)*, 76 *(130)*
superelevation on curves, *18(19-20)*, 36 *(53)*, 39
switches, elec (or pushbuttons), *42 (63C), 43 (64)*, 44 *(65-8)*, *74 (122)*, 90, *90 (147C, 148C)*, 92 *(150N)*, 93
switches, track, *(see* turnouts)

track, trackwork: components, 9, *10 (11)*, 37-41, *37 (54), 39 (55-6), 40 (57-8), 41 (59-61), 42 (62-3);* detection, 74; flexible, *15 (15), 18 (19-20)*, 38; sectional or snap, *10 (11), 16 (16)*, 38
trains: British, *6 (4-5), 7 (6)*, 25 *(31)*, 31 *(41)*, 34 *(50)*, 46 *(69)*, 58 *(86), 59 (87)*, 60 *(88)*, 61 *(91), 67 (106)*, 68 *(107)*, 76 *(131)*, 88 *(145);* Cont Eur, *8 (7), 15 (15*, 24 *(29)*, 54 *(79-80). 67 (105)*, 76 *(130). 81 (138);* electric, *7(6), 20(22B), 31(41), 58(86), 67(105-6);* freight (goods), *34(50), 36(53), 47(70), 54(79-80)*, *63(94), 77(131);* industrial, *85(144);* narrow-g, 23 *(24)*, 24 *(29), 59 (87);* N American, *9 (9), 18 (19)*, 36 *(53), 47 (70)*, 52 *(75), 63 (94)*, 73 *(120)*, 85 *(144*, *91 (91), 77(131);* passenger, *6 (4-5), 7 (6)*, 8 *(7)*, 24 *(29)*, 2 *(31)*, 31 *(41)*, 34 *(50)*, 46 *(69), 47 (70)*, 60 *(88)*, 61 *(91), 67 (105-6)*, 68 *(107)*, 73 *(120)*, 76 *(130)*, 77 *(131)*, 81 *(138)*, 88 *(145);* types of, 86-7
transistors, transformers, *(see* controllers)
transition curves, *21 (23B)*, 22, 39
trees, *8 (7-8)*, 18 *(20)*, 31 *(41), 47 (70), 57 (85)*, 58 *(86), 63 (95), 67 (105)*
traversers, 25-6, *25 (30), 41 (61)*, 56
trestles, 29, *29 (37V)*
tunnels, *21(23), 23(24-5)*, 24(26-7), 36(53), 48, *49(71G), 54(79)*, 55, *55(81A-M), 58(86), 67(106)*, *77(131)*
turnouts, *20 (22), 25 (30 3WT)*, 39-42, *40 (57-8), 41 (59-60), 42 (63), 43 (64)*
turntables, *18 (20), 21 (23)*, 22, 27 *(34)*, 29 *(35E)*, 56, *64 (98)*